W9-BJB-275

Afghanistan

Afghanistan

BY MIRIAM GREENBLATT

*Enchantment of the World
Second Series*

Children's Press®

A Division of Scholastic Inc.

NEW YORK TORONTO LONDON AUCKLAND SYDNEY
MEXICO CITY NEW DELHI HONG KONG
DANBURY, CONNECTICUT

Frontispiece: Fruit stall in Kabul

Consultant: Mohammad Basheer, Center for Afghanistan Studies, University of Nebraska at Omaha

Please note: All statistics are as up-to-date as possible at the time of publication.

Book production by Herman Adler Design

Library of Congress Cataloging-in-Publication Data

Greenblatt, Miriam.
  Afghanistan / Miriam Greenblatt
      p. cm.— (Enchantment of the world. Second series.)
  Includes bibliographical references and index.
  ISBN 0-516-22696-7
  Afghanistan—Juvenile literature. [1. Afghanistan.] I. Title. II. Series.
  DS351.5.G73 2003
  958.1—dc21   2002156471

CHILDREN'S PRESS and associated logos are trademarks and or registered
trademarks of Scholastic Library Publishing. SCHOLASTIC and associated logos
are trademarks and or registered trademarks of Scholastic Inc.
2 3 4 5 6 7 8 9 10 R 12 11 10 09 08 07 06 05 04

Acknowledgments

I would like to thank Tamim Ansary, an Afghan-American with whom I was fortunate enough to work on a textbook on world geography and cultures in 1993. I would also like to thank the many American journalists who went to Afghanistan in 2001 and 2002 and, at the risk of their own lives, sent back hundreds of stories about this far-off land in the heart of Asia.

Cover photo:
Panjshir River
Valley

Contents

Goat herder

Afghan woman

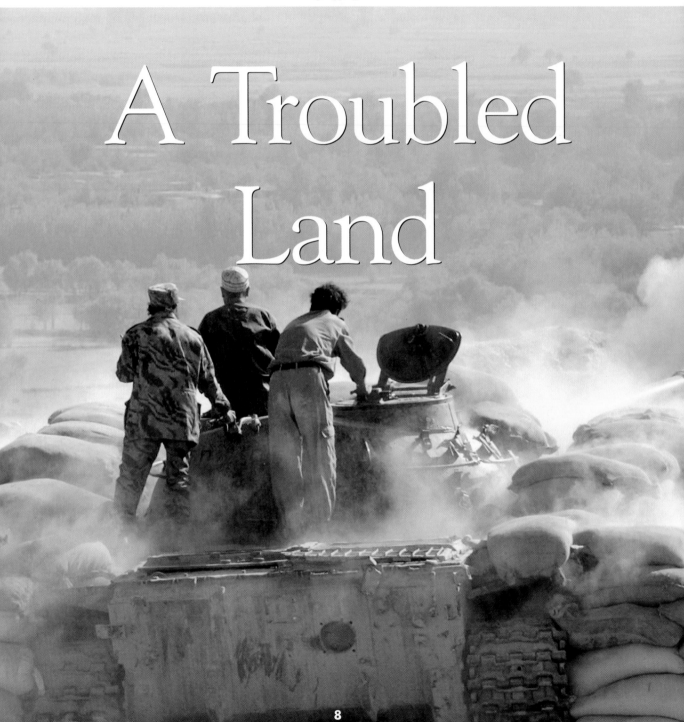

A Troubled Land

IN THE PAST, MOST WESTERNERS ASSOCIATED AFGHANISTAN with adventure stories. In *The Man Who Would Be King*, Rudyard Kipling writes about two British con men who go to Kafiristan—really Afghanistan—and set up their own kingdom. In the first of George Fraser's nine books about Flashman, his hero survives an Afghan siege and is later trapped with British troops in the Khyber Pass between Afghanistan and Pakistan. Ian Fleming's James Bond pursues a villain in Afghanistan's mountains. There would have been no Sherlock Holmes stories by Sir Arthur Conan Doyle if Dr. John H. Watson, an army surgeon, had not been wounded in Afghanistan. After being discharged from the British army, Watson goes home to London, where he and Holmes meet. In all these adventure stories, Afghanistan is portrayed as an exotic, romantic place where men perform heroic deeds and everything seems larger than life.

In November 2001, Americans saw a very different picture of Afghanistan. A journalist named Tim Weiner was in the Afghan city of Jalalabad. One morning he and photographer Stephen Crowley stopped several passers-by. Crowley took their pictures. Weiner spoke with them

Opposite: **Afghan Northern Alliance soldiers shell the Taliban in northern Afghanistan.**

A damaged roof after it was hit by a U.S. bomb raid in July 2002.

This Afghan girl collects garbage to earn extra money for her family.

while the negatives were being developed. Among the passersby were a boy named Abdul Haq, a girl named Brekhna, and a teenager named Ahmad Fawad.

Abdul Haq did not know how old he was. "My father was killed in the fighting years ago," he said. "We had no money, so I started working for my uncle, who stitches shoes. Last year I got my own shoeshine box and polish and started working. I get three Pakistani rupees a shine [about 5 cents]. I don't have money for school, so I work. I would love to go."

Brekhna was nine years old. "I love school but I have no money to buy books and go to school now. I pick garbage. I get plastic. It's useful. I walk an hour from my home to go work. I have heard the noises of the bombs at night. I start crying. My mother hugs me, but I can't sleep."

Ahmad Fawad was eighteen years old. "I'm from Kabul. I heard the news that there was peace in Jalalabad and I came looking for work. I'm a carpenter. My father was a carpenter too. . . . I have not seen peace in my whole life. From childhood I have seen blood, bullets, guns, nothing else. If there is peace, and they want me to build houses, I'm ready to work night and day."

Afghanistan has experienced warfare through most of its history. Sometimes the war has involved Afghans resisting foreign invaders. At other times, it has involved one Afghan tribe fighting another. Since 1979, it has been both. The Afghans are brave and tough people. Perhaps, with enough help from other countries, they will be able to create a peaceful and productive nation. In this nation, refugees can return to their homes and fields, and children can attend school.

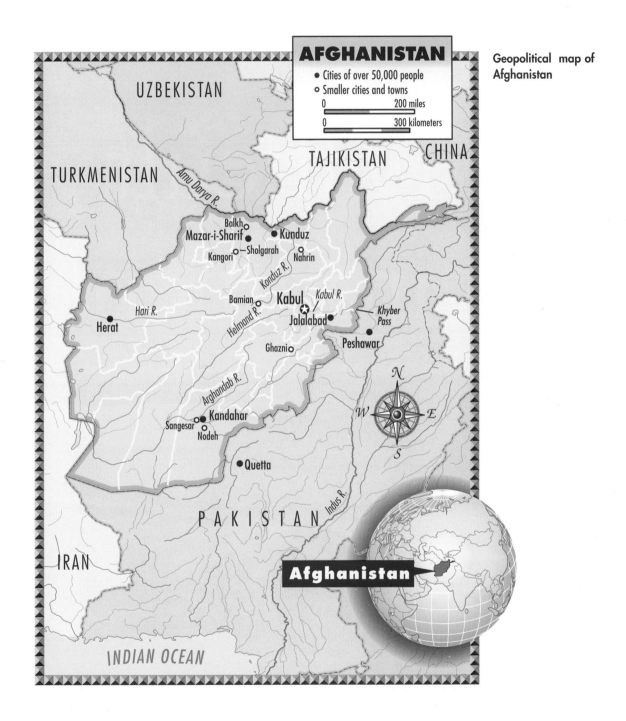

AFGHANISTAN
- Cities of over 50,000 people
- Smaller cities and towns

| 0 | 200 miles |
| 0 | 300 kilometers |

UZBEKISTAN

TURKMENISTAN

TAJIKISTAN

CHINA

Amu Darya R.

Balkh
Mazar-i-Sharif • • Kunduz
Kangori ○ —Sholgarah
Nahrin

Konduz R.

Hari R.

Bamian
Helmand R.
Kabul ☆
Kabul R.
Jalalabad •
Khyber Pass

Herat •

Ghazni ○
Peshawar •

Arghandab R.

N
W E
S

Sangesar ○ • Kandahar
○ Nodeh

• Quetta

Indus R.

P A K I S T A N

IRAN

INDIAN OCEAN

Afghanistan

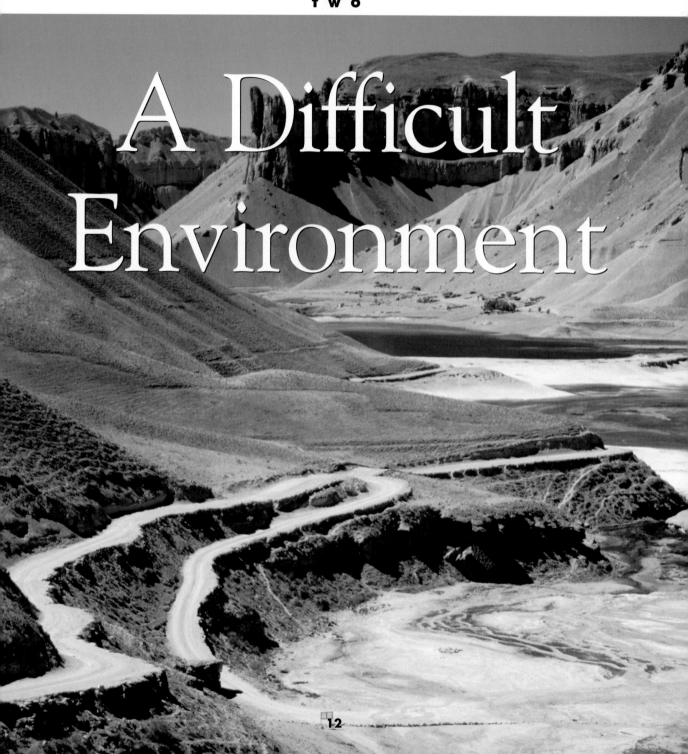

CHAPTER

TWO

A Difficult
Environment

AFGHANISTAN IS A LAND OF TOWERING MOUNTAINS, valleys that look like ribbons of green, and vast deserts of sand or stone. In some places it is very beautiful. In other places it is dry, rugged, and extremely difficult to live in.

Afghanistan is a medium-sized country in south-central Asia. Its total land area is about 251,825 square miles (652,225 square kilometers), making it slightly smaller than the state of Texas. Afghanistan is landlocked. It is bordered on the north by three nations that were formerly part of the Soviet Union: Turkmenistan, Uzbekistan, and Tajikistan. To the northeast, a tiny piece of Afghanistan touches the People's Republic of China. The country shares its eastern and southern borders with Pakistan and its western border with Iran.

Opposite: **A road winds through a rugged valley.**

Snowcapped mountains of the Hindu Kush form a backdrop to the capital city of Kabul.

Three Regions

About two-thirds of Afghanistan consists of mountain ranges. The most massive is the Hindu Kush. Its highest peaks tower more than 20,000 feet (6,000 meters) above sea level and are covered with snow year-round. The name *Hindu Kush* means "Indian killer." In the past, armies invading the Indian subcontinent would bring young boys and girls back

The Khyber Pass, in addition to being an entry point for invading armies, has been a major trade route for centuries.

as slaves. The Indians were not accustomed to high altitudes and bitter cold, however, and they died by the thousands. The most famous pass through the Hindu Kush is the Khyber Pass between Afghanistan and Pakistan.

The Hindu Kush and the smaller ranges that fan out from it divide Afghanistan into three regions: the northern plains, the central highlands, and the southwestern plateau.

Crops grow with the help of irrigation on the northern plains of Afghanistan.

These hillside caves were once used by Buddhist monks.

The northern plains region slopes from the mountains down to the Amu Darya River (formerly known as the Oxus River). When water is available, this is the most fertile part of Afghanistan. Farmers grow crops with the help of irrigation. Herds of livestock graze on the pasturelands. The region also contains large mineral resources.

The central highlands region consists of treeless cliffs broken by the deep, narrow valleys where most Afghans live. The cliffs are honeycombed with hundreds of caves. The northeastern part of the region is very active geologically. Major earthquakes occur about every ten years.

Earthquakes!

In recent years, major earthquakes have been hitting Afghanistan more and more often. In 1998, some 5,000 Afghans were killed in a quake that measured 6.9 on the Richter scale. The quake created cracks in the earth that were 100 feet (30.4 m) wide, 50 feet (15.2 m) deep, and as much as 1 mile (1.6 km) long.

Four years later, on March 3, 2002, Afghanistan suffered an earthquake that measured 7.2 on the Richter scale. Because the quake was deep in the ground, it did not cause as much damage as a shallower quake would have. Nevertheless, about 1,000 houses collapsed, killing about 150 people.

"We all ran," said Abdul Qudos. "Those people who could not get out of their houses were buried."

The quake even affected nearby nations. People in India, Pakistan, Tajikistan, and Uzbekistan felt the ground move beneath them. The walls of buildings and electric poles swayed from side to side.

On March 25, 2002, another major quake hit Afghanistan. This quake measured 6.1 on the Richter scale. The town of Nahrin was flattened, and some eighty nearby villages were severely damaged. About 1,000 people died, and up to 20,000 people became homeless.

Bibi Gul described her experience this way: "I was sitting next to the stove when everything started shaking. Then the house collapsed and the stove was on top of me."

It took 24 hours before rescuers were able to reach Gul. By that time, heat from the stove had burned the skin on her face black.

The southwestern plateau region consists of two deserts divided by a river valley. The river is the Helmand. North of the Helmand is a stony desert called the Sistan Desert. Clumps of camel grass and other thorny plants are the only vegetation that grows there. South of the Helmand is a sandy desert called the Registan. It is full of sand dunes as tall as 100 feet (30 m).

Fields in the Helmand Valley

Four Rivers

The Helmand is the longest river in Afghanistan. It rises in the central mountains and flows southwest for 900 miles (1,448 km). Salt-free for most of its length, the Helmand usually floods in spring and creates marshes and shallow lakes. Its largest tributary is the Arghandab River, which provides water for the cities of Ghazni and Kandahar.

The Amu Darya River rises in the northeastern mountains and flows for 700 miles (1,100 km) along Afghanistan's northern border. It eventually empties into Turkmenistan's Aral Sea. The main Afghan cities near the Amu Darya are Kunduz and Mazar-i-Sharif.

The Hari River rises in the central mountains and flows west for 400 miles (640 km). It then turns north and flows along the Afghan-Iranian border for a distance of 65 miles (104 km) before entering Turkmenistan. The main city near the Hari River is Herat.

The Kabul River, like the Helmand and the Hari, rises in the central mountains. From there it flows east for 380 miles (600 km) into Pakistan's Indus River, which in turn empties into the Arabian Sea. The main cities along the Kabul River are Kabul—the capital of Afghanistan—and Jalalabad.

The Kabul River runs dry during a drought.

Afghan winters are cold and harsh.

Climate

Afghanistan generally has very cold winters and very hot summers. Temperatures range from -24° Fahrenheit (-31° Celsius) in January to 120°F (48.8°C) in July. The southwestern deserts also experience a big difference between daytime and nighttime temperatures. A high of 100°F (37.7°C) at noon often drops below freezing after the sun goes down.

Most of Afghanistan is covered with snow from November through March. In general, however, the country is extremely dry. The average rainfall measures just 13 inches (33 centimeters) per year. This varies from a high of 53 inches (135 cm) in the east to a low of 3 inches (8 cm) in the southwest.

The southwestern plateau is also noted for the *bad-i-sad-o-bist-roz*, the "wind of 120 days." This wind blows from June through September and often reaches speeds of 100 miles (160 km) per hour. It shifts sand dunes from place to place, with columns of sand swirling across the land.

Drought!

Lack of rain is a major environmental problem in Afghanistan. A severe drought hit the country (as well as other parts of Asia) in 1998 and was still continuing in 2002. As one observer wrote, "Soil and seeds have blown away, vegetation has baked brown, livestock have been slaughtered, and wells and rivers have run dry.... Cities and villages have instituted water rationing."

The drought has affected not just the growing of food and the raising of livestock. It is also causing political problems with Afghanistan's northern neighbors—Tajikistan, Uzbekistan, and Turkmenistan. All four nations draw water from the Amu Darya, and each nation resents the amount of water that goes to the others. A similar dry spell helped bring about the overthrow of a previous Afghan government in 1973. This drought might do the same.

Afghanistan's Geographic Features

Highest Elevation: Mount Nowshak, 24,557 feet (7,485 m)

Lowest Elevation: 1,640 feet (500 m) above sea level in the Sistan Desert

Greatest Distance North to South: 630 miles (1,012 km)

Greatest Distance East to West: 820 miles (1,320 km)

Longest River: Helmand, 900 miles (1,448 km)

Largest Lake: Lake Saberi

Longest Mountain Chain: Hindu Kush, 700 miles (1,100 km)

Largest City (2002 est.): Kabul, 2,600,000

Highest Average Temperature: 120°F (48.8°C) in Jalalabad

Lowest Average Temperature: -24°F (-31°C) in the central highlands

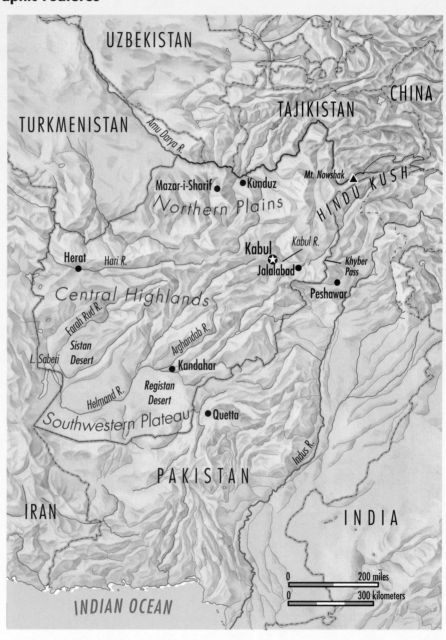

Forests, Flowers, Animals, and Plants

Land once farmed is now useless because of the destruction caused by bombs.

T HE WARFARE THAT HAS DEVASTATED AFGHANISTAN SINCE 1979 has severely damaged its environment. Bombs set numerous forest fires. Millions of refugees polluted water supplies as they moved across the country. If the refugees brought their livestock with them, the animals overgrazed the pasture-lands. More and more people were armed with guns, and they killed more and more animals for food. It will be years before conservation efforts improve the situation.

Opposite: **Though Afghanistan is almost treeless, trees line this road in Bamian Valley.**

Forests, Flowers, Animals, and Plants **23**

Afghanistan has almost no trees. Only about 1 to 3 percent of the land is forested. Afghans have chopped down most of their trees to use for firewood. Trees also were burned during the recent wars. Pine and fir trees are found in the high mountains. Cedar, oak, walnut, and juniper trees grow at lower altitudes. Afghans particularly value a type of cedar that they use to make furniture.

A grove of poplars in the Bamian Mountains.

Anemones are one of several flowers found in Afghanistan.

The country's shrubs include currant, gooseberry, hawthorn, honeysuckle, and rose. Among the flowers that bloom in spring are the anemone and the cowslip. These are followed by lilies and tulips, which are followed in turn by dahlias, geraniums, marigolds, and sunflowers.

The most common domesticated animals in Afghanistan are sheep, cattle, and goats. They provide people with meat

A goat herder tends his flock.

Camels are often used to transport hay across the desert.

and milk. For transport, Afghans use donkeys, horses, mules, and camels. The camels are of two kinds: the one-humped dromedary, which is found on the plains, and the two-humped Bactrian camel, which lives in the mountains.

The Ibex

The ibex is a wild goat. The male has a dark brown coat with whitish patches on its belly and back. Its thick, ridged horns curve for an average length of 53 inches (135 cm). The female ibex has a light tan coat.

In summer the ibex migrate high up into the mountains to graze. Females and their offspring usually live in groups of ten to twenty animals. Males live in separate groups that spend a considerable amount of time fighting. First the ibex rear up on their hind legs. Then they charge their opponents and smash their heads and horns together. In winter the ibex move lower down the mountains, and males, females, and offspring live together.

Different animals thrive in different parts of Afghanistan. The northern plains region is home to a ground squirrel called the suslik. At one time large numbers of Siberian tigers lived along the Amu Darya River, but most of them have been shot by hunters. The central highlands region contains wild sheep, brown bears, wolves, foxes, and snow leopards. Gazelles roam the southwestern plateau region.

Two animals native to Afghanistan have become popular pets in many Western countries. One is the so-called Persian cat, which is noted for its long, silky fur. The Persian has a wide head, and its legs and tail are short. It comes in many colors, including grey, blue, red, cream, and white.

The suslik, or ground squirrel

The Persian cat comes in several different colors.

The Afghan hound's coat is long and silky.

The other is the Afghan hound. It is an elegant, long-legged dog with droopy ears. The Afghan hound is a very fast runner. Afghans often use it to track down prey when they go hunting.

Afghanistan's skies are filled with almost 400 different species of birds. There are birds of prey, including eagles, falcons, hawks, and vultures. Game birds include pheasants, quail, and the red-legged shukar partridge. Afghans often breed this partridge for fighting. There are eighty different kinds of wild pigeons and doves. Among the more common songbirds are larks, nightingales, and blue jays. In the fall,

waterfowl migrating from Siberia stop in Afghanistan on their way to Arabia or India. Flamingos thrive in marshy areas.

Fish are plentiful in Afghanistan's rivers and streams. They include carp, salmon, sturgeon, and trout. The most common shellfish is the freshwater crab.

Doves take flight in the courtyard of the Hazrat Ali shrine in Mazar-i-Sharif.

Protecting the Environment

In January 2003, a press conference was held by Ahmad Yusuf Nuristani, the Afghan minister for irrigation, water resources, and environment, and Pekka Haavisto of the United Nations. The two men warned about the increasing dangers to Afghanistan's environment.

Desert sands are swallowing up hundreds of villages. The country's pistachio forests are half their former size. Wildlife is disappearing. For example, the Siberian cranes that once migrated to India by way of Afghanistan have not been seen since 1986. Worst of all, perhaps, is the smuggling of timber across the border to Pakistan. Although the Afghan government has stopped the cutting of trees in eastern Afghanistan, there are not enough policemen to control the illegal border trade.

Mr. Nuristani proposed a budget of $8 million for 2003. However, it is questionable whether the Afghan cabinet will approve his request because the country has so many other financial needs.

CHAPTER

FOUR

A Turbulent History

AFGHANISTAN LIES AT THE CROSSROADS OF TWO GREAT trade routes. One is the east-west route between Europe and China. The other is the north-south route between central Asia and India. Because of its location, Afghanistan has been invaded over and over through the centuries. Among the invaders have been the Persians, the Greeks, the Arabs, the Mongols, the British, and the Russians.

Invaders have not been the country's only problem. Afghanistan has struggled hard to develop a sense of national unity among its different ethnic groups. Most Afghans are still far more loyal to their tribe than to their nation.

Opposite: **Afghanistan is a country plagued by centuries of invasions. In Kabul, people walk by the ruined palace of a former prime minister.**

Early Civilization

By 6000 B.C.E., the early inhabitants of Afghanistan had domesticated animals and had learned how to grow wheat and barley. By 3000 B.C.E. they were living in a series of small towns scattered throughout the southern part of the country. These people grew cotton and made black-on-red pottery. They traded with Egypt and Iraq to the west and with India to the southeast.

Around 1500 B.C.E., groups of nomadic herders known as Indo-Aryans began migrating into Afghanistan and settling in the northern part of the country. The newcomers brought with them several languages. These included present-day Afghanistan's two national languages, Pashto (also spelled Pushtu) and Dari.

Above left: **Zoroaster, founder of Zoroastrianism**

Above right: **Today most worshippers of Ahura Mazda live in India and Iran.**

Bottom: **An image of Ahriman**

About 600 B.C.E., a man named Zoroaster introduced a new religion. He taught that Ahura Mazda, or God, had created everything that was good in the world. Opposing him was a spirit named Ahriman, who had created everything that was evil. Ahura Mazda and Ahriman were constantly battling each

other. Zoroaster urged people to show their support of Ahura Mazda by speaking the truth, helping the poor, and trying to make the world a better place. Anyone who was greedy, lazy, or proud was a supporter of Ahriman. Eventually a Judgment Day would come, and Ahura Mazda would triumph over Ahriman. This new religion, which is still followed today, is called Zoroastrianism, after its founder.

About 540 B.C.E., northern Afghanistan—then called Bactria—was conquered by the Persians under Cyrus the Great. He spread Zoroastrianism throughout his empire. By 500 B.C.E., Cyrus's son Darius I had extended the empire's boundaries to include all of present-day Afghanistan.

Darius I built the first great highway system in the world.

The Rule of the Greeks

In 329 B.C.E., one of the world's greatest conquerors invaded Afghanistan. Named Alexander the Great, he was a Macedonian from the area north of Greece. It took him just two years to conquer Afghanistan and to establish a Greek colonial empire that was to last for 200 years.

After conquering Afghanistan, Alexander married a beautiful woman named Roxane, the

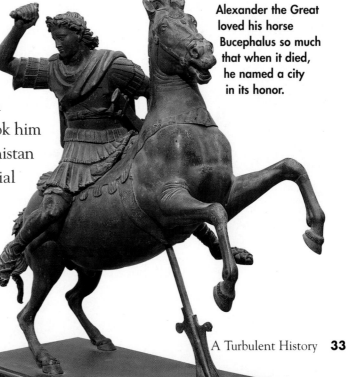

Alexander the Great loved his horse Bucephalus so much that when it died, he named a city in its honor.

daughter of a Bactrian chief. The marriage probably happened for political reasons, but Afghans like to tell folk stories about Alexander's romance with Roxane. Roxane (or Rukhsana) is still a popular name for Afghan girls.

After Alexander died in 323 B.C.E., three of his generals fought for power among themselves. Afghanistan fell into the hands of Seleucus. About 304 B.C.E. Seleucus was defeated in battle by an Indian king named Chandragupta Maurya, who took over the southern part of the country.

A fourth-century statue of Siddhartha Gautama

The Coming of Buddhism

The Mauryan dynasty, or family of rulers, brought Afghanistan another new religion. Its founder, Siddhartha Gautama, is known as the Buddha, or Enlightened One. The religion is known as Buddhism.

Buddhism developed out of another religion, Hinduism. A basic belief of Hinduism is reincarnation. It means that people's souls are continually reborn, each time in a different body. This belief troubled Siddhartha. Why did people have to suffer and grow old, sicken, and die time after time?

After years of wandering and meditating, Siddhartha was enlightened. He realized that the way for people to avoid rebirth was by overcoming selfishness and becoming one with God. The way to overcome selfishness was to follow the Noble Eightfold Path. The path included keeping an open mind; speaking the truth; not hurting another person or an animal; and working not for material things that belong only to one-self, but rather for things that belong to everyone, such as peace.

The Mauryas ruled southern Afghanistan for more than one hundred years. During this time, large numbers of Greek colonists continued to settle in Bactria. In 185 B.C.E., the Mauryan dynasty collapsed. The Bactrian Greeks promptly moved south and took over most of Afghanistan.

At about the same time, tribes of nomads began migrating westward from central Asia, probably because of drought. As they moved westward, they pushed other tribes ahead of them. One of these was the Sakas, who pushed the Greeks out of Bactria and took it over. Soon afterward, however, the Sakas themselves were pushed out by another tribe from central Asia, the Kushans.

The Rule of the Kushans

After establishing themselves in Bactria, the Kushans proceeded to conquer southern Afghanistan. Then they combined the cultures they had conquered with their own. They converted to Buddhism. They adopted the writing script and coinage of the Greeks. They also adopted Greek techniques in art and created magnificent statues and paintings of the Buddha.

An ivory Kushan statue

Inscription in the Kushan language using Greek letters

A Turbulent History **35**

Camels transport goods along the Silk Road.

By the middle of the first century C.E., the Kushan Empire was flourishing. Kushan missionaries carried Buddhism into China and Mongolia. The trade route known as the Silk Road, which linked China with Rome, wound across Afghanistan. Archaeologists digging near Kabul have found objects made of Chinese lacquer, ivory from India, Roman bronze, and painted glass from Egypt.

In 220, the Kushan dynasty came to an end and Afghanistan split into several kingdoms. For a time much of the country was again ruled by the Persians. In 400, another wave of nomads from central Asia, the White Huns, overran Bactria. In 565, the Persians took control of Afghanistan yet again.

Then, in 652, a new group of invaders arrived. They brought yet another new religion, Islam. These newcomers were the Arabs.

The Arab Invasion

Afghans have many legends about the Arab invasion. One is the story of the two-sworded king. He was a great warrior who fought with a sword in each hand. During the battle for Kabul, an Afghan soldier cut off the king's head. Instead of falling dead, the king put his head under his arm and kept on fighting.

The Arabs lost control of Afghanistan soon after conquering it. Islam, however, gradually replaced Buddhism as the popular religion. Today, almost every Afghan is a Muslim, or follower of Islam. You will learn about the teachings of Islam in chapter 8.

After Arab rule in Afghanistan ended, the country was controlled by three native dynasties in succession: the Tahirids, the Saffarids, and the Samanids. Then, in 962, a Turkish slave named Alptigin (or Aliptagin) overthrew his Samanid master and founded a new dynasty, the Ghaznavid.

The Rule of the Ghaznavids

The leading Ghaznavid king, Mahmud of Ghazni, was the dynasty's third ruler. Mahmud was a great military leader who extended the boundaries of his empire from Persia to the Ganges River in India. He completed the conversion of the Afghans to Islam. A patron of the arts, Mahmud filled his capital city of Ghazni with magnificent palaces, gardens, monuments, and mosques (Muslim houses of worship). Some of the buildings were made of baked brick, others of marble.

Hundreds of artists, poets, and scholars flocked to his court. Among them was the renowned Persian poet Ferdosi.

After Mahmud died in 1030, the Ghaznavid Empire declined. In 1150, it was conquered by the Ghorids, who lived in the mountains east of Herat. The Ghorids burned Ghazni and set up their capital at Herat.

The Rule of the Mongols

In the early 1200s, one of the most devastating events in Afghan history took place. The armies of Genghis Khan poured out of Mongolia and swept across central Asia. In Afghanistan they leveled Herat and massacred all its inhabitants, including the animals. They dumped the books from the library in Balkh into the Amu Darya River. According to

Mongol warriors created the world's largest land empire.

Famous Travelers

During the period of Mongol rule, two world travelers visited Afghanistan and wrote about what they saw. The first traveler was Marco Polo (1254?–1324?) (right). He crossed Afghanistan on his way from Venice to the court of Kublai Khan, Genghis Khan's grandson, in Cambalue (now known as Beijing, China). Polo commented on many things that are still found in Afghanistan. They include almond and pistachio nuts, "innumerable quantity of sheep," "the very best melons in the world . . . sweeter than honey," and "excellent horses, remarkable for their speed."

The second traveler was Ibn Batuta (1304?–1378?). A native of Morocco, he spent about thirty years visiting such places as India, China, Indonesia, Spain, and West Africa. He described Kabul as a "village inhabited by a tribe of Persians called Afghans." Afghans "hold mountains and defiles [narrow mountain passes] and possess considerable strength, and are mostly highwaymen." It was Ibn Batuta who explained the meaning of Hindu Kush as Indian killer.

legend, there were 1 million volumes, "enough to choke the river." The Mongols plowed salt into Afghanistan's farmland, making it unfit to grow crops. They let the country's wells and irrigation canals fill with sand.

Tamerlane was called "The Lame" because of an old war wound.

For the next hundred or so years, Afghanistan suffered under Mongol control. Then Mongol control weakened, and Afghanistan became a collection of small states ruled by local chiefs. In the late 1370s, another Mongol conqueror arrived. His name was Timur-i-Lang (Timur the Lame), or Tamerlane, and he was a descendant of Genghis Khan. Tamerlane conquered Afghanistan on his way to India and established the Timurid dynasty.

Afghanistan blossomed under the Timurids. They rebuilt Herat and filled it with beautiful mosques. They welcomed architects, calligraphers, musicians, and scholars from all over Asia. New trade routes were opened. The great miniature painter Ustad Kamal al-din Bihzad, who was born in Herat about 1440, worked at the Timurid court before moving to Persia.

Timurid rule in Afghanistan lasted for about one hundred years. Then history repeated itself. The Timurid Empire crumbled, and local warlords set up states of their own, only to be replaced by a new conquerer: Babur.

Babur

Zahir-ud-din Muhammad, nicknamed Babur, meaning "the Tiger," was descended from Genghis Khan on his mother's side and from Tamerlane on his father's. In 1494, at the age of eleven, he became ruler of the kingdom of Ferghana in what is now Uzbekistan. Babur was kicked off the throne seven years later. He then moved south with a few hundred followers. By the age of twenty-one, he had conquered eastern Afghanistan and had set up his capital at Kabul. He spent the next twenty years conquering the rest of Afghanistan and preparing for an attack on India. In 1526 he captured the Indian city of Delhi and founded the Mogul (or Mughal) Empire, which controlled most of India for more than 300 years.

Babur conquered a great deal of territory in spite of being in poor health for much of his life.

Babur loved Kabul. He found its climate and scenery delightful. He enjoyed gardening and spent many hours studying the local plants. He was an accomplished poet, writing in both Dari and Turkic. He also wrote his memoirs, in which he described Kabul as "an excellent and profitable market for commodities. . . . Every year seven, eight, or ten thousand horses arrive in Kabul. From Hindustan [northern India] every year fifteen, twenty thousand pieces of cloth are brought by caravans. . . . There are many merchants who are not satisfied with getting three or four hundred percent."

Babur died in 1530. He was later buried in Kabul, in a garden he had planted himself. Afghans still make pilgrimages to visit his tomb.

Nader Shah

A Time of Change

The next two centuries were full of upheaval for the Afghans. They found themselves caught in a power struggle between the Moguls to the south, the Persians to the west, and the Uzbeks to the north. Borders shifted frequently. Herat, Kabul, and Kandahar changed hands over and over again.

In the early 1700s, a group of Afghan tribes took control of part of the Persian Empire. In the 1730s, a former slave and goat herder named Nader Quli Beg (later known as Nader Shah) began rising to power. First he drove the Afghans out of Persia and seized the Persian throne. Then he conquered Afghanistan itself. Next he marched on Delhi, where he looted the treasures of the Moguls, including the Koh-i-noor diamond and the jewel-encrusted Peacock Throne.

Nader Shah was a great general. As time went on, however, he grew increasingly suspicious of everyone around him. He even had his own son blinded because he suspected the youth of wanting to seize power. He may have been going mad. In any event, in 1747 he was assassinated by members of his bodyguard.

The commander of Nader Shah's bodyguard was an Afghan named Ahmad Khan Abdali. The night Nader Shah was assassinated, Ahmad Khan left the Persian camp with 4,000 Afghan soldiers and went to Kandahar. There he took the title of Durri Durrani, or "pearl of the age," and set about turning Afghanistan into an independent country.

It was a discouraging task. The various Afghan tribes were far more used to fighting one another than they were to cooperating. Afghanistan was poor, and the only way Ahmad Khan could get money was by invading and looting India. Nevertheless, he succeeded in establishing an empire that stretched from India to Persia and from the Amu Darya River to the Arabian Sea. He dealt with the various Afghan tribes by allowing the chief of each tribe to handle his own tribe's affairs. All the chiefs formed a *jirga*, or council, that gave Ahmad Khan advice. Ahmad Khan reformed Afghanistan's criminal code and encouraged the arts. Today Afghans regard him as *Ahmad Shah Baabaa*, the "Father of the Nation."

Ahmad Khan's empire did not last long after his death in 1773. Different Durrani princes claimed the throne and fought one another instead of focusing on how to govern Afghanistan. Finally, in 1818, a man named Dost Muhammad Khan came on the scene. First he defeated Shah Shuja, the Durrani king. Then he declared war against northern India. This last act was a big mistake.

Background of the Great Game

Afghanistan's location was significant for India. Afghanistan could block an invasion from the north. On the other hand, it could launch an invasion itself. In the past, the main outsiders with interest in Afghanistan had included the Greeks, the Persians, the Arabs, and the Mongols. Now, as Europeans developed sea routes for trade with Asia, new players appeared.

First came the British. In 1600, Queen Elizabeth I gave the East India Company the right to trade in India. By the mid-1700s France, Portugal, and Holland had followed Britain. The four European nations competed with one another for trade and political influence. Britain was the most successful.

Beginning in the early 1700s, Russia started looking for warm-water ports that would enable it to trade year round. Russia expanded east across Siberia to the Pacific Ocean and moved into present-day Alaska and California. It also moved south toward India and Persia. By 1800, as one historian wrote, "Russia and Great Britain were about to clash in what has been called the Great Game of power politics." Unfortunately, Afghanistan would be caught in the middle.

The Great Game

When Dost Muhammad Khan declared war against northern India, he asked the British for help. The British refused. They did not trust the Afghans, and besides, they wanted northern India for themselves. Dost Muhammad then asked the Russians for help. Alarmed by this act, the British invaded Afghanistan.

The First Anglo-Afghan War lasted from 1838 to 1842. The British captured Ghazni, Kabul, and Kandahar and

Central Asia, 1900

Russian Empire	British territory
Russian sphere of influence	Allied w. British
	British sphere of influence

British troops on the march to Kabul in the First Anglo-Afghan War in 1838

placed the former king, Shah Shuja, on the throne. The Afghans hated Shah Shuja, however, and refused to obey him. The Afghans launched attack after attack against Kabul until at last the British decided to withdraw. Some 4,000 soldiers and 12,500 camp followers set out through the snow and cold of the mountains. Before they could reach Jalalabad, most of them were massacred by Afghan hill tribes. It was one of the worst defeats ever suffered by a colonial power.

Dost Muhammad, who had been in exile, returned to Afghanistan and ruled for the next twenty-one years. He was succeeded in 1868 by his third son, Sher Ali Khan.

Ten years later, the Second Anglo-Afghan War broke out. It lasted from 1878 to 1880. It began when Sher Ali Khan welcomed a Russian diplomatic mission to Kabul but refused to allow a British countermission to cross the border. Furious at the insult, the British invaded Afghanistan and drove Sher Ali out of the country. He died in 1879.

In 1880, the British gave control of Afghanistan—except for its foreign affairs—to Sirdar Abdur Rahman Khan, nephew of Sher Ali and grandson of Dost Muhammad. In some ways it was a good choice. During his reign, which lasted from 1880 to 1901, Abdur Rahman took several important steps toward unifying his country. He established a strong national army. He crushed a number of tribal revolts and moved loyal tribesmen into the rebellious areas. He set up a national system of courts.

On the other hand, Abdur Rahman was not interested in modernizing Afghanistan. He rejected both the railway and the telegraph. He also rejected foreign experts who wanted to help improve the Afghan economy.

It was during Abdur Rahman's reign that the British and the Russians decided where Afghanistan's present boundaries were to be. The southern boundary—known as the Durand Line—split the land inhabited by Afghanistan's major ethnic group, the Pushtuns. Ever since, many Pushtuns have called for creation of a new nation to be called Pushtunistan. It would include all the areas where Pushtuns live, namely, parts of Afghanistan and Pakistan (formerly northwestern India).

Afghanistan's next king was Abdur Rahman's eldest son, Habibullah, who ruled from 1901 to 1919. Unlike his father, Habibullah took several steps toward modernization. He abolished slavery. He built Afghanistan's first hospital. He established a high school, a military academy, and a teacher-training college—all run like European schools.

Then came World War I. Habibullah kept his country neutral. This angered many religious and tribal leaders who supported Turkey's call for a *jihad*, or Muslim holy war, against Britain. In 1919, while out hunting, Habibullah was murdered, apparently by jihad supporters.

Pushtunistan

////// Predominant Pushtun area
▨ Maximum claimed area of Pushtunistan

Habibullah was succeeded by his third son, Amanullah. Because so many Afghans were agitating for complete independence from Britain, Amanullah decided in 1920 to invade India, most of which was under British control. The Third Anglo-Afghan War lasted just one month. However, the peace treaty was not signed until 1921. Under the treaty, Britain gave up control over Afghanistan's foreign affairs. Afghanistan was now truly independent.

Attempts at Modernization

Like his father, King Amanullah worked hard to modernize his country. He introduced its first constitution. He replaced tribal law codes with a secular, or nonreligious, national code. He founded schools that both boys and girls could attend. He said it was all right for women to stop covering their faces with veils.

Amanullah's actions infuriated the country's conservative religious leaders and their followers. In 1928, the eastern and southern tribes revolted, and Amanullah was forced from the throne. After nine months of terror and chaos, a man named Muhammad Nadir Khan, a relative of Amanullah, was declared king.

Nadir Shah, as Nadir Khan became known, concentrated on strengthening Afghanistan's central government. He enlarged the army and set up an assembly representing all the tribes. To soften religious opposition, he ordered women to veil their faces. He also replaced Amanullah's secular law code with a code based on *sharia*, or Islamic law.

In 1933, Nadir Shah was assassinated, and his son Muhammad Zahir Shah became king. Zahir Shah undertook several reforms, such as founding the University of Kabul and making Pashto a national language. He built new highways and set up a national bank. After World War II, however, Zahir Shah began to run into trouble. He encouraged construction of two large dams in the Helmand Valley to bring water to southwestern Afghanistan for agriculture. The project leaders ignored the saltiness of the water and the thinness of the local soil. They also ignored villagers' resistance to modern farming techniques. The result was a failure that cost Afghanistan millions of dollars.

In 1953, Zahir Shah's cousin, Mohammad Daoud Khan, became prime minister. With financial support from Russia, then known as the Soviet Union, Daoud pushed for more modernization. He built up the army and expanded the educational system. He also encouraged women to unveil their faces and to appear in public. However, he was dismissed in 1963 after a war scare with Pakistan.

In 1964, Zahir Shah approved a new constitution. It provided for a two-house legislature, many of whose members were elected rather than being appointed by the king. The elections, which were held in 1965, marked the first time women could vote. Unfortunately, the king and the legislature disagreed about almost everything. To make matters worse, a severe drought hit the country in 1971–1972. As many as 100,000 people died.

Finally, in 1973, Daoud, with the army's help, overthrew Zahir Shah. Daoud then declared Afghanistan a republic, with himself as president.

For the next five years, Daoud ran Afghanistan with an iron hand. He gave jobs only to his relatives and friends. He allowed only one political party to exist. At the same time, he tried to improve the nation's economy. He nationalized banks and distributed land to people who had none.

In 1977, Daoud changed his approach. Instead of obtaining aid from the Soviet Union, he turned to Saudi Arabia and Iran (formerly Persia). Instead of working with pro-Soviet politicians, he appointed a cabinet of extreme political and religious conservatives. Alarmed at these actions, the pro-Soviet commanders of his military and air force staged a coup and assassinated Daoud in April 1978. The coup is known as the *Saur*, or "April," Revolution.

Enter the Soviet Union

The country's new leaders moved quickly to establish communism and to gain support from the Afghan people. They called for land reform. They proposed universal elementary education, as well as an adult literacy program. They abolished the tradition of dowries for marriages and forbade the charging of interest on loans. At the same time, they killed or imprisoned large numbers of military officers, clergy, and professionals who disagreed with their ideas. Thousands of Soviet advisers arrived to help run the government.

The result was a series of rebellions throughout Afghanistan. Tribal chiefs declared their independence. Fundamentalist Muslim leaders called for a religious revolu-

Soviet troops in Afghanistan

tion. City dwellers demanded an end to mass executions. Villagers objected to the adult literacy program because it would include women. Farmers who had received land but no access to irrigation water lost their crops and turned against the government. Soldiers deserted from the Afghan army. The situation grew more and more chaotic. Finally, in December 1979, Soviet troops invaded Afghanistan. They killed the country's president and put in a regime that they controlled.

The resulting war lasted ten years. Many Soviet soldiers had received only a few months of training. They were unprepared for fighting in mountains and on desert plateaus. As many

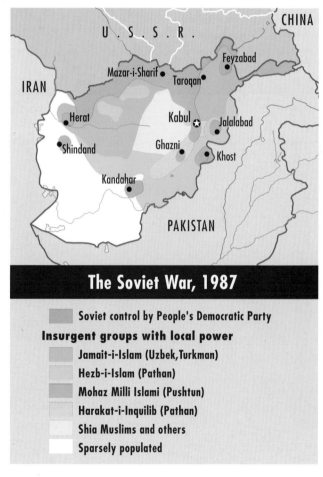

The Soviet War, 1987

- Soviet control by People's Democratic Party

Insurgent groups with local power
- Jamait-i-Islam (Uzbek, Turkman)
- Hezb-i-Islam (Pathan)
- Mohaz Milli Islami (Pushtun)
- Harakat-i-Inquilib (Pathan)
- Shia Muslims and others
- Sparsely populated

as three in four soldiers came down with hepatitis. About one in three came down with typhoid.

In the meantime, various Afghan tribes joined together to form the mujahedin resistance movement. The word *mujahedin* means "those fighting a Muslim holy war." The mujahedin began a campaign of guerrilla warfare. They damaged roads and communications and took over many local governments. Some mujahedin operated from Afghanistan's mountains. Others operated from bases in Iran and Pakistan. They received weapons from such anti-Soviet nations as the United States, China, and Saudi Arabia.

Mujahedin fighters received military aid from nearly twenty nations.

The war devastated Afghanistan. Like the Mongols in the 1200s, the Soviets destroyed forests and irrigation systems, burned crops, and killed farm animals. Between 5 and 6 million Afghans became refugees, mostly in Iran and Pakistan. For their part, the mujahedin killed or wounded about 50,000 Soviets. The mujahedin were also merciless to any Afghan they suspected of helping the Soviets or even of accepting their presence. Khakim Tilaev, a Soviet soldier who fought in Afghanistan from 1984 to 1987, tells the following story:

I saw a woman...with her hands and legs cut off and her eyes put out, because her two sons had helped the Soviets. They killed the rest of her family. But they left her alive to suffer, and so all of the other people could see what could happen to anyone who worked with us.

Afghanistan's cities were a major target of the fighting during the 1980s and 1990s.

At last, the Soviet Union decided it had had enough. The war was hurting its relations with Muslim countries. The war was also very expensive and highly unpopular with the Soviet people. In February 1989, the Soviet Union withdrew its troops.

Enter the Taliban

The Soviet withdrawal left Afghanistan divided. A pro-Soviet government controlled the cities, while the mujahedin controlled the countryside. The civil war between the two groups lasted more than three years. In April 1992, the mujahedin captured Kabul.

The mujahedin victory, however, did not bring peace to Afghanistan. The mujahedin contained several major factions: fundamentalist Islamic groups, moderate regional groups, supporters of the exiled king, and varied ethnic groups. Each group had its own vision of what Afghanistan should be like in the future, and each group wanted to be in charge. In addition, foreigners supporting their favorite faction pushed their own agendas.

The struggle for control continued. Conditions within Afghanistan went from bad to worse as warlords tore the country apart. In 1994, a new player appeared on the scene: the Taliban. It was led by a *mullah*, or Islamic cleric, named Muhammad

The Taliban, which took over most of Afghanistan in the late 1990s, imposed a tough code of conduct on Afghanistan's people, especially the women.

Omar Akhund—Mullah Omar for short. The word *Talib* means "religious student," and many members of the Taliban had been students at *madrassas*, or religious schools, in the Afghan refugee camps in Pakistan. Saudi Arabia supplied the Taliban with money and manpower. Pakistan also supplied manpower, as well as weapons and military advice.

Gradually the Taliban, which refused to work with the mujahedin, took over more and more of Afghanistan. By 1998, it controlled about 85 to 90 percent of the country. Afghans welcomed the regime at first because it brought some peace and security. The Taliban crushed warring tribal groups and took away people's guns. It also opened the roads between Afghanistan, Iran, and Pakistan. This allowed people to carry on the drug trade on which the Afghan economy had become dependent.

On the other hand, the Taliban imposed a very strict interpretation of Islam. Thieves had their hands or feet amputated. People were required to attend prayers at their local mosque. Women were forbidden to work or to go to school. If they went out of the house, they had to wear a *burka*. A burka is a long, pleated bag that covers a woman from head to toe.

Afghan women could not go out in public unless covered in a burka.

Mullah Muhammad Omar Akhund

Mullah Omar was born in either 1959 or 1961 in the village of Nodeh, near Kandahar. After studying at a madrassa, he moved to the village of Sangesar, also near Kandahar, where he became the local mullah. Between 1989 and 1992, he fought with the mujahedin. He lost his right eye in the course of the fighting, which gave him the nickname *rund*, or "one-eyed."

After the mujahedin victory, he returned to Sangesar.

In 1994, Mullah Omar set out to lead a jihad. His goal, as he saw it, was not to grab power, but rather to cleanse Afghan society and re-establish the rule of Sharia. Although shy and a poor public speaker, he was joined by thousands of fighters, many of them Arabs and Pakistanis.

A mesh strip at eye level allows her to see where she is going. However, the lack of ventilation may make her nauseated. Also, it is hard for her to hear anything that is going on around her.

The Taliban banned all sorts of activities that it considered un-Islamic, such as flying kites; playing chess; keeping pigeons or other birds as pets; dancing at weddings; playing a musical instrument; hanging paintings, photographs, or portraits in the home or office; watching television; using a computer; going to the movies; singing lullabies to babies; women wearing high heels; and men wearing neckties. A religious police force saw to it that everyone obeyed the rules.

Osama bin Laden

Osama bin Laden

Among the foreigners who arrived in the 1980s to help the mujahedin was a student from Saudi Arabia named Osama bin Laden. Osama used engineers and equipment from his father's construction company to build roads and storage facilities for the mujahedin. He also set up an organization called *al Qaeda*, or "military base," to help the Arab-Afghans fighting in Afghanistan.

In 1990, Osama returned home. Soon afterward, war broke out in the Persian Gulf region. Iraq invaded Kuwait and was apparently preparing to attack Saudi Arabia. Osama tried to convince the Saudi king to use Arab-Afghan war veterans to fight Iraq and to protect Saudi oil reserves. Instead, the king invited in troops from the United States. Osama was horrified. Why were non-Muslims allowed to have military bases in the country of Islam's holy city of Mecca? He was even more horrified when American troops remained in Saudi Arabia after Iraq's defeat in 1991. Osama criticized the Saudi royal family for allowing the Americans to stay and called for a jihad to liberate his homeland. The royal family responded by taking away his citizenship.

In 1996, Osama bin Laden returned to Afghanistan. The following year, he moved to Kandahar, where he and Mullah Omar became very friendly. The Taliban leader promised to protect Osama and to provide a base for al Qaeda. Osama supported the Taliban with Arab-Afghan fighters and money.

Money was no problem for Osama. Al Qaeda collected hundreds of millions of dollars from Muslim individuals and organizations around the world. Some of the money went to fundamentalist Islamic groups in various countries, including Sudan, Egypt, and Algeria in Africa and in Asia, Pakistan, Bangladesh, and the Philippines. The rest of the money was used to mount terrorist attacks against the United States. In 1993, bombs were exploded in the basement of the World Trade Center in New York City. In 1998, American embassies in Kenya and Tanzania were attacked. More than 250 people were killed, and 5,000 were wounded.

The climax came on September 11, 2001. Al Qaeda members hijacked four airplanes in the United States. Two of the planes rammed into the twin towers of the World Trade Center in New York, which collapsed. One plane crashed into the Pentagon in Washington, D.C. The fourth plane, which was supposed to hit the White House, was apparently taken over by its passengers before diving into the ground in Pennsylvania. More than 3,000 people died. It was one of the worst terrorist attacks in world history.

Enter the United States

On October 7, 2001, American and British airplanes and cruise missiles hit Afghanistan. The attack was designed to destroy the terrorist training camps of al Qaeda and the Taliban. American commandos, as well as soldiers from Britain and several other nations, landed on the ground in Afghanistan. They joined up with the Northern Alliance, a collection of groups that had been resisting the Taliban since 1994.

During the next few months, the Northern Alliance took over Afghanistan. Some Taliban fighters surrendered, while others melted into the general population. A large number fled to Pakistan. A few retreated to caves in the central highlands to carry on guerrilla warfare. Both Osama bin Laden and Mullah Omar disappeared.

Bombed bunker used by al Qaeda

In December, four Afghan factions met in Bonn, Germany, and formed an interim government for their country. Heading the government, which was to last for six months, was a man named Hamid Karzai. In June 2002, Afghanistan held a *loya jirga*, or grand council, chaired by the country's former king, Muhammad Zahir Shah. Despite clashes between competing warlords and disagreements among ethnic groups, the loya jirga succeeded in setting up a transitional government. It is expected to rule for up to two years. Then nationwide elections will be held.

Delegates from various Afghan factions gather in Bonn, Germany, after signing an accord for an interim government.

Choosing the Loya Jirga

The loya jirga that met in June 2002 was made up of 1,501 people. It included 1,051 delegates chosen by tribal elders from candidates in each city and village. In addition, about 400 seats were reserved for women, nomads, members of the clergy, and Afghan refugees living in Iran and Pakistan. Seats were also assigned to intellectuals, artists, traders, and journalists. A few seats were saved for Sikhs and Hindus.

Participants in the loya jirga had to be over twenty-two-years old and know how to read and write. They could not have a criminal record or be connected with a terrorist organization. Anyone who had caused civilian deaths, either directly or indirectly, was not eligible. However, a number of warlords, drug lords, and politicians used threats and bribery to make certain that they or their supporters were chosen.

A Transitional Government

T HE LOYA JIRGA HELD IN June 2002 was an extraordinary event in Afghan history. As two of the delegates observed, "Delegates from all backgrounds . . . urban and rural; Sunni and Shiite—sat together under one roof as if we belonged to a single village. Men and women mingled openly and comfortably. . . . We were living proof against the stereotypes that Afghans are . . . a backward people not ready for

Afghan women delegates discuss the formation of a new legislative body during the loya jirga.

democracy and equality." Although the immediate results of the loya jirga were minor, the meeting set an example for the country. "We still believe that the seeds of democracy planted by the loya jirga will take root and flourish. . . . [T]he popular will of Afghans will not tolerate a retreat into the past."

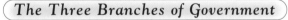

The Three Branches of Government

The transitional government in Afghanistan consists of three branches: executive, legislative, and judicial. It will run the country until elections for a permanent government are held in 2004.

Opposite: **Afghan president Hamid Karzai addresses the loya jirga.**

Afghanistan's Flag

Afghanistan adopted a new flag in 2002. Based on the old royal flag first used in 1928, it contains three equal vertical sections. From left to right, they are colored black, red, and green. The middle of the red section shows the nation's coat of arms in gold. In addition to a mosque and a pair of flags, the coat of arms includes two religious phrases in Arabic script. One phrase is *Allah o Akbar* or "God is Great."

The other phrase is "There is no God but Allah, and Muhammad is the Prophet of Allah."

The executive branch is headed by President Hamid Karzai, who was elected by the loya jirga. The executive branch also includes five vice presidents, appointed by Karzai. More vice presidents were to be appointed later.

Delegates to the loya jirga were unable to decide on the structure of the Afghan legislature. Some delegates argued in favor of having two representatives from each of the country's thirty-two provinces. (This is similar to the U.S. Senate.) Other delegates supported the idea of giving more seats to provinces with a larger population. (This is similar to the U.S. House of Representatives.) The first model would give more power to the Pushtuns. The second model would give more power to urban centers, such as Kabul.

Delegates were also unable to agree as to the function of the legislature. Some delegates

TRANSITIONAL GOVERNMENT OF AFGHANISTAN

Executive Branch

PRESIDENT

VICE PRESIDENTS (5)

Legislative Branch

Judicial Branch

Hamid Karzai

Hamid Karzai was born in 1957 in Kandahar. His father, a prominent Pushtun, was chief of the 500,000-member Popolzai tribe and also a speaker of the Afghan Parliament under King Zahir Shah.

Karzai attended high school in Kabul. When the Soviet Union invaded Afghanistan in 1979 he went to Simla, India. There he obtained a master's degree in political science and learned to speak English fluently. Karzai also speaks Pashto, Dari, and four other Afghan languages.

After graduating from university, Karzai became an intermediary during the mujahedin war against the Soviet Union. He obtained money, weapons, and supplies—apparently from the United States—and sent them to the mujahedin. After the Soviets withdrew from Afghanistan, he served for two years as deputy foreign minister in the mujahedin government. He grew increasingly upset over the constant fighting among the warlords and the corruption of many mujahedin leaders. In 1994, he became a supporter of the Taliban. "The Taliban were good, honest people," he said. "I had no reservations about helping them." After several months, however, he realized that the Taliban movement was being taken over by Pakistanis and Arabs. In 1996, he went into exile in the city of Quetta, in western Pakistan. By 1998, Karzai was encouraging open rebellion against the Taliban.

In 1999, Karzai's father was killed in Quetta on his way home from evening prayers in the mosque. The Karzai family blamed the Taliban. Two years later, Karzai slipped across the border to lead the anti-Taliban movement in southern Afghanistan. It was a

brave thing to do. At one point the Taliban succeeded in tracking him down. Only an American air strike prevented his being captured and hanged.

In December 2001, Karzai was chosen to be the head of Afghanistan's interim government. In June 2002, he was elected president of the transitional government.

Karzai is married to a doctor. He and his wife, Zenat, have no children. Six of Karzai's seven siblings live in the United States. Some are teachers; others operate a chain of Afghan restaurants called Helmand, after the province west of Kandahar.

felt it should be purely an advisory body. Others argued that it should have the power to enact laws and to approve budgets. Karzai said that the judiciary would operate under a legal code based on sharia.

Major Problems

Two major governmental problems face Afghanistan today. The first is how to please the country's different ethnic groups. The second is how to strengthen the central government.

The two main ethnic groups in Afghanistan are the Pushtuns and the Tajiks. Ever since Ahmad Khan Durrani founded the kindom of Afghanistan in 1747, the country had been ruled mostly by Pushtuns. However, the Northern Alliance, which played a major role in defeating the Taliban, was made up mostly of Tajiks. When the interim government was established at Bonn in 2001, it was dominated by Tajiks. They headed the key departments of defense, foreign affairs, and interior—this means they controlled the army and the police. The cabinet appointed by Hamid Karzai in 2002 was more balanced. The defense minister remained a Tajik, but the post of interior minister went to a Pushtun. Representatives of two other ethnic groups, the Hazaras and the Uzbeks, also received top government positions.

In order to strengthen the central government, Hamid Karzai appointed several leading warlords as vice presidents. He hoped the move would weaken the warlords' control over their regions, since they would have to serve in Kabul. Two other warlords refused to become vice presidents unless they could keep their regional power bases. The two are Ismail Khan of Herat, and Uzbek leader Abdul Rashid Dostum of Mazar-i-Sharif.

Hamid Karzai has much more to do in order to create a strong central government. He has to develop a national army that can control the private armies of the warlords. He has to balance the demands of fundamentalist mullahs who support an Islamic state with the need to protect the rights of women in social and political affairs. He has a tremendous job ahead of him.

In addition to these governmental tasks, Hamid Karzai faces another problem: staying alive. In February 2002, his minister for aviation and tourism was attacked by a mob at the Kabul airport and beaten to death. In April, the defense minister narrowly escaped death when a bomb exploded near his car in Jalalabad. In July, one of Karzai's vice presidents was killed in Kabul by gunmen who lurked outside his office. Karzai himself was the object of an assassination attempt in September. He was riding in a car through a crowd of well-wishers in Kandahar. A gunman stepped in front of the car and started firing. Two bullets barely missed Karzai. The gunman was killed by Karzai's bodyguards.

"I've been through this before," Karzai said after the attack. "My father was assassinated . . . by the Taliban, by terrorists. Did that stop me from fighting against them? . . . I will not stop. I will continue."

Kabul: Did You Know This?

Kabul became Afghanistan's capital in 1776. It is the nation's largest city by far. Kabul lies in a narrow fertile valley about 6,000 feet (1,828 m) above sea level. Bare, rocky mountains rise to the west and south. The city has lots of sunshine and an invigorating climate. It is rainy in spring but dry in summer. Winter snows are heavy, and the city is often snowbound for weeks at a time. The air in Kabul used to be clear, but large numbers of refugees, as well as exhaust fumes from military trucks, have caused severe air pollution.

The Kabul River flows through the city's center. The old part of Kabul lies on the south bank of the river. Here you find flat-roofed houses built of mud brick, narrow alleys, and covered markets called bazaars. There are no street signs or house numbers. As one observer wrote, "If you don't know where you are going, you probably have no business here." The modern part of Kabul lies on the north bank of the river. Here you find government and commercial buildings, banks, and schools. The streets are wide and paved with asphalt. Two- and three-story buildings contain apartments above a ground floor of shops.

About half of Kabul was reduced to rubble during the years of fighting. More than 70 percent of the artwork in the famed Kabul Museum was either destroyed or stolen and sold abroad. Only a few animals are still alive in the Kabul Zoo.

Population (2002 est.): 2.6 million
Average daily temperature: 76°F (24.4°C) in July; 23°F (-5°C) in January
Average annual rainfall: 13 inches (33.8 cm)

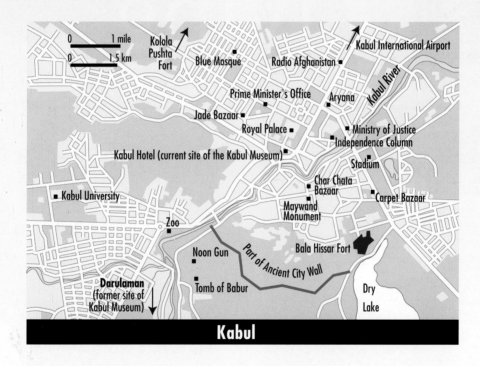

Kabul

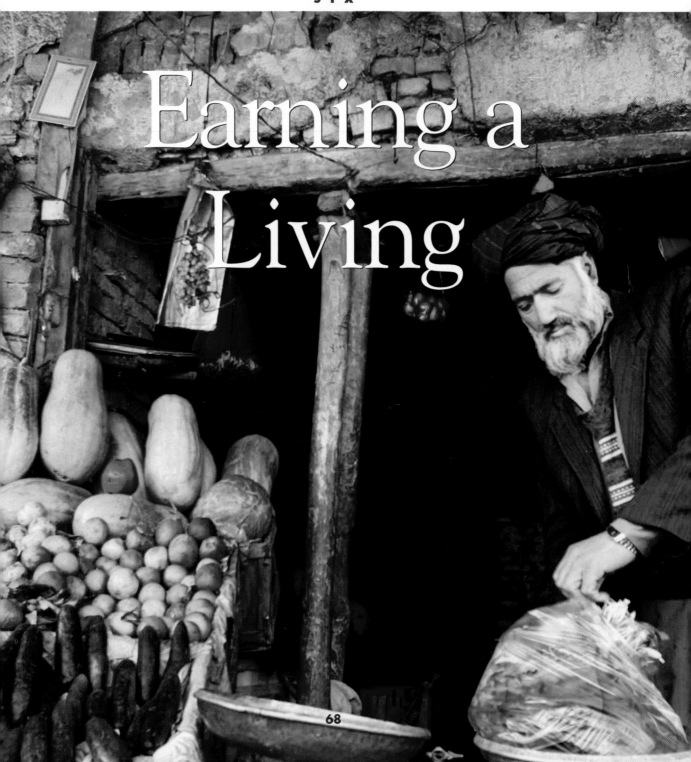

CHAPTER SIX

Earning a Living

AFGHANISTAN IS ONE OF THE POOREST COUNTRIES IN the world. Although it has many natural resources, they have not been developed. Years of warfare have devastated farms, factories, buildings, and roads. The movement of soldiers and refugees also has damaged the country. There are few doctors and fewer hospitals. As a result, the average life expectancy of Afghans is only about forty-six years. About one out of every four rural children dies before the age of five.

Farming and Herding

Most Afghans earn their living by farming. However, only 12 percent of the country's land can be tilled. The rest is too rugged for cultivation. Another difficulty is the shortage of

Watercourses are few and far between in Afghanistan.

Earning a Living **69**

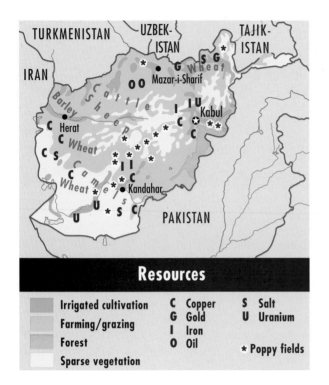

Resources

▓	Irrigated cultivation	C	Copper	S	Salt
▓	Farming/grazing	G	Gold	U	Uranium
▓	Forest	I	Iron		
░	Sparse vegetation	O	Oil	*	Poppy fields

water. More than half of the available farmland has to be irrigated in order to grow crops. Some of the water for irrigation comes from the country's rivers. Some comes from snowmelt in the mountains. Afghan farmers bring the snowmelt to their fields by means of underground canals.

Farming methods in Afghanistan are generally primitive. Many farmers still use wooden plows pulled by oxen. They rarely fertilize their fields or choose seeds in a scientific manner. They harvest their crops by hand.

Most Afghan farmers lack money to buy tractors and other modern farming equipment.

A Plague of Locusts

In the summer of 2002, an unusual type of war broke out in northern Afghanistan. It was a war against the worst attack of locusts in more than thirty years.

Locusts hatch in the mountains in spring and immediately start eating their way down the mountainsides. By summer, when they are about 2 inches (5.08 cm) long, the orange-legged insects reach the valleys. There they take wing, filling the air with a steady buzz. It has been estimated that a swarm of locusts can devour a wheat field in less than four hours. If the insects enter a city, they form such large drifts in the streets that cars skid off the slick surface.

Under the Soviet regime, Afghan farmers received pesticides to kill the locusts. As the Soviets withdrew, the pesticide program collapsed because farmers could not afford to pay for it. During the years of mujahedin government, there was so much fighting among various factions that farmers either abandoned their fields or were unable to spend time fighting the insects. The Taliban proclaimed that killing locusts violated the teachings of Islam. "This is a living creature, the creation of God, and you should not kill it. God alone is charged with giving food."

In 2002, the United Nations Food and Agriculture Organization (FAO) mounted a campaign against locusts. It sent teams of men on motorcycles into the mountains to find the locust hatchlings and kill them. The workers dug 10-inch (25.4- cm) deep trenches (above) for miles around the pastures where the locusts had laid their eggs the previous year. The workers used blankets and plastic sheets to beat the young locusts into the trenches, which were then covered with dirt. The FAO also set up a spraying program.

In all, the FAO managed to save about 90 percent of northern Afghanistan's food and fiber crops. It hopes to be even more successful in 2003.

Growing poppies is a lucrative business in Afghanistan.

Afghanistan's leading crop is wheat. Other food crops include barley, corn, rice, sugar beets, fruits, and nuts. Some farmers raise cotton for textiles. Cottonseed is made into oil and soap.

Afghanistan's biggest cash crop is opium, which comes from the opium poppy and is used to make heroin and other narcotics. Growing poppies yields about ten times the profit that growing wheat does. It also requires only half the amount of water.

The Taliban at first encouraged poppy cultivation because it brought in a lot of money. During their last year in power, they banned poppy cultivation and managed to cut production by about 95 percent. The ban left several hundred thousand farmers without jobs or food. Some tried to keep going by borrowing money even though it left them in debt for years to come. Others sought refuge in Iran and Pakistan. In the fall of 2001, when the Taliban was under attack, Afghanistan's farmers again planted poppy seeds. The new interim government likewise banned poppy cultivation, in January 2002, but by then it was too late. The new crop was already sprouting.

The United States and several European nations suggested buying up the poppy harvest and destroying it. This idea was abandoned, however, because officials felt it would only encourage farmers to plant poppies again the following year. The United States and Britain then suggested paying farmers to plow under their fields. However, the amount of the suggested payments was not high enough to persuade farmers to destroy the crop. It remains to be seen what the new Afghan government can do to stop poppy cultivation.

About 1 to 2 million Afghans, especially in the south, are nomadic herders. Other Afghans call them *kochis*—"people who move." They travel in bands of up to 100 people. In summer they take their flocks of goats and fat-tailed sheep up into the mountains. In winter they come down the mountains into the sheltered valleys. The animals furnish meat and fat for food and skins and wool for clothing. The nomads trade or sell their products for grain, vegetables, and fruits grown by farmers.

Young nomadic shepherds

A Hungry Land

Twenty-three years of war and five years of drought have created a serious food shortage in Afghanistan. At the beginning of 2002, it was estimated that two out of three Afghans were suffering from malnutrition. At least 5 million Afghans were starving. Many had nothing to eat but wild spinach and blades of grass. The situation was so bad that some Afghan families sold their children for bags of wheat.

"What else could I do?" asked Akhtar Muhammad, who lives in the village of Kangori. He had already sold his farm animals, his family's rugs, and his family's metal cooking utensils. Finally, he took two of his sons—a 10-year-old boy named Sher and a 5-year-old boy named Baz—to the bazaar in the nearby town of Sholgarah. There he traded Sher for forty-six pounds of wheat per month for six years. For Baz, he got twenty-three pounds of wheat per month for six years.

"I miss my sons," Muhammad said, "but there was nothing to eat." Muhammad still has eight children at home to feed.

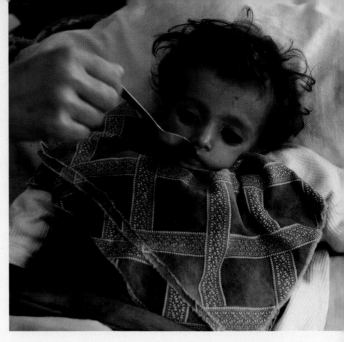

Six weeks after selling Sher, Muhammad came across his son in a crowded street. The two hugged each other, and Muhammad asked Sher how he was getting along with the family that had bought him.

"They don't treat me well," Sher replied sadly. "I work very hard and during the night they send me into the mountains to sleep with the sheep. I felt bad that I was sold. I cried. Sometimes I still cry. I cry at night. But I understand why the selling of me was necessary."

Handicrafts

Afghanistan is famous for its handwoven carpets. Some are made of wool, others of cotton or silk. Dyes for the thread come from wildflowers and herbs. Weavers often work together in teams of four. It takes a team three months to make a rug measuring 2 feet (61 cm) by 3 feet (91.5 cm). Most weavers are female. Afghan men pay a high bride price for women who are expert weavers.

Afghan men are skilled metalworkers. They make such farming tools as horseshoes, knives, plows, and sickles out of iron. Coppersmiths turn out jugs, pots, and trays. Silversmiths and goldsmiths produce necklaces and bracelets. Many Afghan women wear their family's wealth in the form of jewelry.

Another popular craft is that of leathermaker. Afghan men are noted for making round or peaked hats out of the skins of karakul sheep. The most common colors are gray and black. Only very important men wear hats that are yellow or brown.

A blacksmith heats a tool over an open flame.

Mining and Manufacturing

Lapis lazuli from Afghanistan was used by the ancient Greeks more than 3,000 years ago.

Afghanistan is rich in minerals, especially iron ore and natural gas. Iron ore is difficult to mine because the deposits are in a remote part of the country and there are no roads. Natural gas makes up about 40 percent of the country's exports. Other minerals known to exist include coal, copper, lead, and zinc. These deposits have not yet been developed, however.

Afghanistan produces most of the world's lapis lazuli. This is a blue semi-precious stone that is made into jewelry. Other valuable stones and gems include amethysts, emeralds, rubies, tourmalines, and jade.

Afghanistan has great potential for hydroelectric power. In spring the country's rivers and streams fill with water from melting snow. To date, however, electric power plants have been built only in the large cities. Rural areas do not have electricity.

Most industries in Afghanistan are small. There are mills for ginning cotton and weaving textiles. Factories make cement from limestone and fertilizers out of nitrogen. There are plants that refine sugar and process fruits. Other plants turn out such products as ceramics, shoes, and soap.

Afghan women work at a textile factory in northern Afghanistan.

What Afghanistan Grows, Makes, and Mines

Agriculture

Wheat	2,499,000 metric tons
Grapes	330,000 metric tons
Corn	240,000 metric tons

Manufacturing

Food products	7,041,000 metric tons
Textiles	324,000 metric tons
Cement	120,000 metric tons

Mining

Natural gas	3,000,000,000 cubic meters
Salt	13,000 metric tons
Copper	5,000 metric tons

Pipe Dreams

A large part of the world's reserves of oil and natural gas lies in Turkmenistan. Presently, the only oil and gas pipelines from Turkmenistan run to Russia. Since 1995, there has been a campaign to build additional pipelines through Afghanistan to Pakistani ports on the Indian Ocean. Building these new pipelines would bring an estimated $500 million to Afghanistan. The country could also earn at least $50 million a year from transit fees.

There are two problems, however. The first is competition between central Asian nations and Western oil companies, especially several from the United States, as to who will build the pipelines. Second, the pipelines would run through remote mountainous areas of Afghanistan, where regional warlords have more power than the central government. The warlords might destroy the pipelines if the government did not bribe them.

Tourism

One industry that has tremendous potential in Afghanistan is tourism. Trekkers could walk or ride along the old caravan trade routes. Bird-watchers could observe migrating birds. Hundreds of caves containing paintings from the life of the Buddha fill the mountains around Bamian. Mazar-i-Sharif boasts the beautiful Blue Mosque. A citadel of Alexander the Great towers over Herat. Babur's tomb lies in Kabul.

For tourism to take root, Afghanistan needs peace and a stable central government. The country also would need to improve its airline service and build good hotels where tourists could stay.

Transportation and Communication

People in rural areas of Afghanistan get around on foot or on horseback. People in cities use buses and bicycles. Almost no one owns an automobile.

Afghanistan has about 13,660 miles (21,000 km) of highways. About 13 percent are paved. They form a great circle connecting Kabul with other cities such as Jalalabad, Ghazni, Kandahar, Herat, and Mazar-i-Sharif. Unfortunately, most of the highways have been severely damaged by war and negligence. One reporter describes them as follows: "With potholes large enough to topple even the largest trucks, blasted bridges that lie in a tangled mess on riverbeds, and a thick carpet of brown dust as fine as talcum powder, the roads are not so much a means of passage as an endurance test." The rest of the country's highways are unpaved and therefore unusable in rainy or snowy weather.

Afghan men on bicycles, the most common form of transportation, make their way into Kabul.

A decorated truck is ready to take to the highway.

Afghans usually travel the highways in trucks, which they often paint in bright colors. Because of the miserable condition of the roads, most trucks are ready for the scrap yard after two years. Afghanistan does not have any railroads of its own. But there are two stretches of railway that are extensions of Uzbek and Turkmen networks.

A Boeing 727 of Ariana
Afghan Airlines performs
a fly-over at Kabul
International Airport.

Afghanistan has two international airports, at Kabul and
Kandahar, and several dozen local airports. The national air-
line owns only two planes, both of which are old and rickety.
It usually offers just two flights a week.

Radio is the most popular means of communication in
Afghanistan. In 1997, there was one radio receiver for every
eleven Afghans. Many receivers were located in the teahouses
of Afghan villages, where men would gather to drink tea and
to exchange news. There was one television set for every 100
Afghans and one telephone for every 862 Afghans.

In April 2002, Afghanistan entered the information age
when the country's first cellular phone service started in
Kabul. By the end of the summer, it was expected that all
provincial capitals would be part of the wireless network.

About twelve newspapers are published in Afghanistan. Most are in Pashto and Dari. Kabul boasts a newspaper in English.

Money Facts

Afghanistan's unit of currency is the afghani. In October 2002, the transitional government issued a new afghani, which is worth one thousand old ones. The new banknotes, which were printed in Germany, have silver strips like the new currency issued by the European Union. The silver strips make it almost impossible to counterfeit the new notes. As of February 3, 2003, 42.7 afghanis were equal to US$1.

Bank of Afghanistan deputy governor Ishaq Turab shows the new afghani in October 2002.

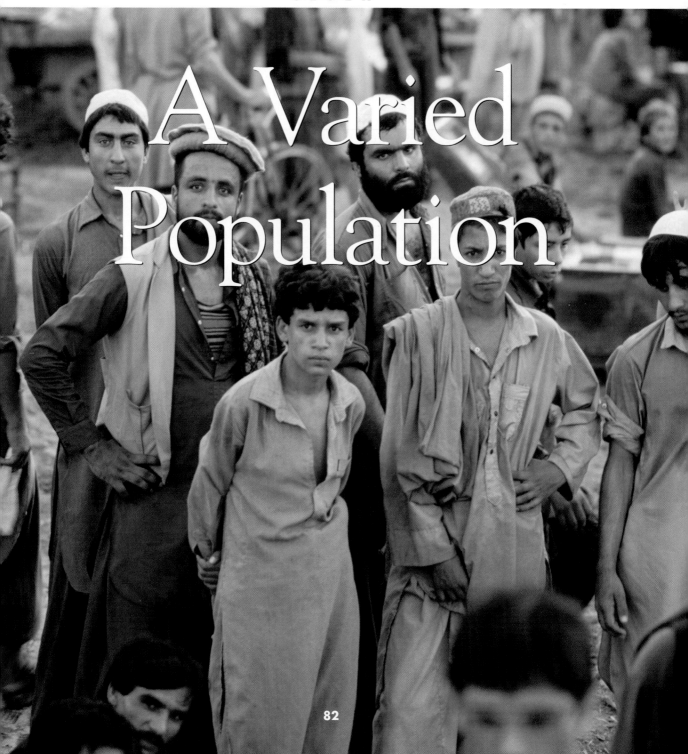

A Varied Population

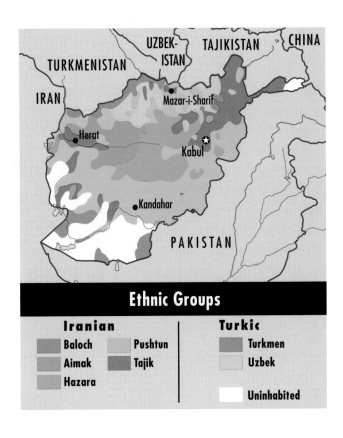

Ethnic Groups

Iranian

- Baloch
- Aimak
- Hazara
- Pushtun
- Tajik

Turkic

- Turkmen
- Uzbek

Uninhabited

As of 2001, it was estimated that Afghanistan's population numbered 26.8 million. It is an extremely varied population. Afghans belong to many different ethnic groups and speak many different languages.

The Pushtuns

About 38 percent of Afghanistan's population are Pushtuns. They live mostly in the south and the east. The Pushtuns have always been the country's dominant ethnic group. Their language of Pashto is one of Afghanistan's two official languages. Afghanistan became an independent nation under Pushtun leadership, and the monarchy that ruled until 1973 was Pushtun. Some 10 to 12 million Pushtuns also live across the border in Pakistan.

Most historians believe that the Pushtuns are descended from the Indo-Aryan tribes that began arriving in Afghanistan around 1500 B.C.E. The Pushtuns themselves have a legend that says they are descended from one of the ten lost tribes of Israel. Supposedly, a grandson of King Saul (the first king of Israel) named Afghana left Israel around 950 B.C.E. and came to Afghanistan with his forty sons.

Ethnic Breakdown in National Population

Pushtun	38%
Tajik	25%
Hazara	19%
Uzbek	6%
Other minorities	12%

Opposite: **Afghanistan contains more than twenty different ethnic groups.**

A Tribal Code

Because the Pushtuns are Afghanistan's leading ethnic group, their tribal code—known as Pushtunwali—is followed by most Afghans. There are three main elements to the code: honor, hospitality, and revenge.

Honor means that people are expected to keep their promises, no matter what the cost. Men are expected to fight bravely and either to win the battle or to die on the battlefield. To Pushtuns, there is nothing lower than a traitor or a coward.

Hospitality means giving food and shelter to anyone who asks. It does not matter if the person is a relative or a stranger, a bitter enemy or a good friend. Afghans are among the most hospitable people in the world.

Revenge means securing justice against anyone who has harmed you or, if that is not possible, against a member of that person's family or tribe. Rules spell out the proper revenge for crimes ranging from stealing cattle to murder. Feuds often continue for generations.

Pushtuns are tall, with light-brown skin, black or brown hair, eyes that are usually brown, and prominent noses. They have a strong fighting tradition. Most Pushtun males either

A Pushtun mujahedin or resistance fighter

Some Common Words in Pashto

lashkar	army
kitab	book
wor-kaey	child
bazgar	farmer
wuz	goat
astogna'h	home
safar	journey
zamin-dar	landowner
ghwasha'h	meat
ghar	mountain
sulha'h	peace
khwar	poor
khub	sleep (n)
obah	water

Major Language Groups

- Pashto
- Dari
- Uzbeki
- Turkmeni
- Baluchi
- Other

carry a gun at all times or keep one in the closet. When a Pushtun male is born, the first thing he hears is often the sound of a gun being fired over his head.

The Tajiks

The second-largest ethnic group are the Tajiks. They make up about 25 percent of the population. Concentrated in the north, they are related to the inhabitants of Tajikistan. In fact, there are more Tajiks living in Afghanistan than there are in Tajikistan.

Tajiks are tall and light-skinned. Their hair is usually black, but sometimes red or blond. Tajiks are mostly farmers, but some live in the cities, where they work as traders, artisans, and government employees. Tajiks speak Dari, the second of Afghanistan's two official languages.

Young Hazara girls

Say It in Dari

Dari is a dialect of Farsi, the official language of Iran. Below are some useful expressions in Dari, along with their English translations as well as a sample of written Dari.

Shomaa chetaur hasted?	How are you?
Aaz amadan-e shomaa, khosh hastam.	I am glad that you have come.
Nam-e shomaa chist?	What is your name?
Khodaa haafez.	Goodbye.
Man na-mefahmam.	I do not understand.
Lotfat aasta boro!	Please drive slowly!
Tashnaab kojast?	Where is the washroom?
Che waqt ast?	What time is it?

دطالبان او القاعده مشراتو
تا ٥ مليون دالر جائزه اُدر مقابل ارائه معلومات
موثق در باره محل بود و باش و يا دستگيری
رهبران طالبان و القاعده پرداخته ميشود.

The Hazaras

The Hazaras make up about 19 percent of Afghanistan's population. With their yellow skin, narrow-lidded eyes, high cheekbones, and little or no facial hair, they are probably descendents of the soldiers of Genghis Khan. They speak a dialect of Dari. In rural areas, they work as shepherds. In the cities, they work as porters and construction laborers. Hazaras are generally disliked by other Afghans. This is partly because of their ancestry and partly because they follow the minority Shi'ite branch of Islam rather than the Sunni branch that most Afghans practice.

The Uzbeks

The Uzbeks, who are related to the inhabitants of Uzbekistan, make up about 6 percent of the Afghan population. Their faces are broad and flat, and they have lighter skin than the Pushtuns. Most Uzbeks are farmers. They also breed horses and karakul sheep. Their language is Uzbeki.

Other Ethnic Groups

The rest of Afghanistan's population consists of fifteen to twenty smaller ethnic groups. The Chahar Aimak are nomadic herders who speak Dari. The Turkmen, like the Hazaras, are of Mongoloid descent. Mostly herders and farmers, Turkmen speak Turkic, which is related to Uzbeki. The Baluch and Brahui are dark-skinned herders who do a lot of smuggling. They speak Baluchi and Pashto. The blue-eyed, fair-skinned Nuristani are probably descended from the soldiers of Alexander the Great. Other groups include the Kazakhs, the Qizil Bash, and the Chagatai Turks.

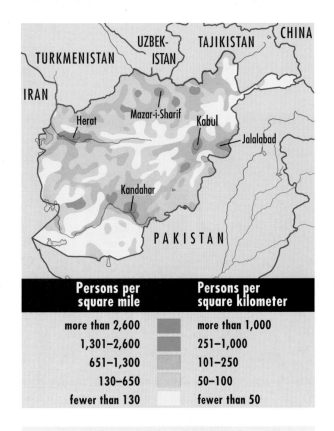

Persons per square mile		Persons per square kilometer
more than 2,600		more than 1,000
1,301–2,600		251–1,000
651–1,300		101–250
130–650		50–100
fewer than 130		fewer than 50

Population of Major Afghan Cities (as of 1988)

Kabul (2002 est.)	2,600,000
Kandahar	225,500
Herat	177,300
Mazar-i-Sharif	130,600

What's in a Name?

Most Afghans have only one official name: their first name. This is the name that appears on their passports and other public documents. If people want to change their official name, they must get permission from the government. Most Afghans also have a tribal name that they use whenever they feel like it. Afghans also add names on the front of their official name. For example, if you make a pilgrimage to the holy city of Mecca, you are called Haji.

The difficulty arises with Afghans' last names. People can choose whatever last name they like. As a result, it turns out that Said Qassim Rishtya and Mir Mohammad Siddiq Farhang are brothers. People can change their last name whenever they want.

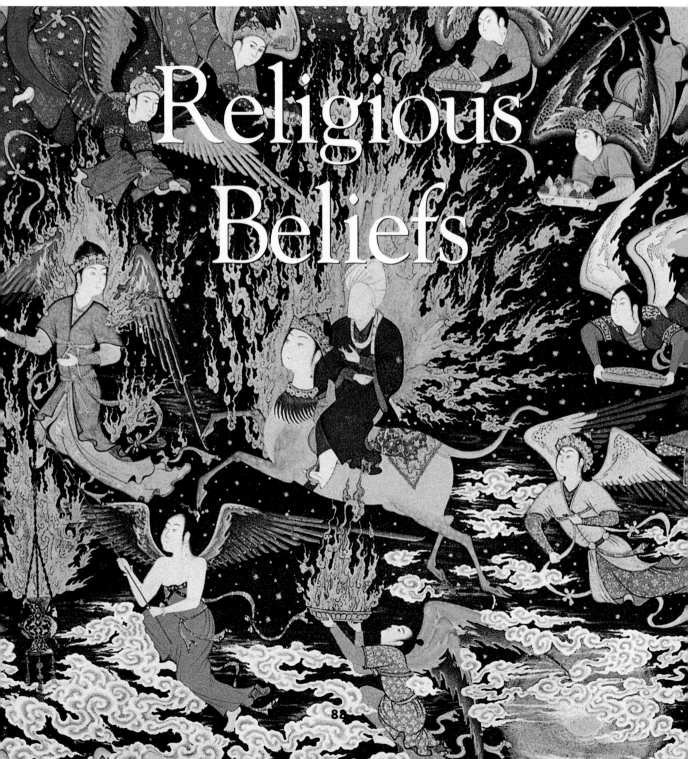

Religious Beliefs

ISLAM, WHICH MEANS "SUBMISSION TO GOD," IS THE YOUNGEST of the world's three major monotheistic religions (Christianity and Judaism are the others). More than 99 percent of the Afghan people are Muslims. The rest are Hindus, Sikhs, and Jews.

Opposite: **"The Ascension of the Prophet Muhammad"**

The Teachings of Muhammad

Islam began in the 600s. According to tradition, an Arab named Muhammad received revelations from Allah, or God,

The angel Gabriel reveals Allah's words to Muhammad.

through the angel Gabriel. The revelations were later written down in the Muslim holy book, the Koran (also spelled Qur'an). Muslims regard Muhammad as the last and greatest of the prophets. Earlier prophets include Noah, Abraham, Moses, David, Solomon, and Jesus.

Muslims have five basic duties, known as the five pillars of faith. The first pillar is believing and reciting the Muslim creed. Every day, Muslims say, "There is no god but God, and Muhammad is the Messenger of God."

Muslims do not ask for favors when praying; instead, they praise Allah.

The second pillar is prayer. Muslims pray five times a day: at sunrise, noon, late afternoon, twilight, and nightfall. The prayers are spoken in Arabic, and Muslims face in the direction of the holy city of Mecca in Saudi Arabia while praying. Women usually pray at home, but men pray in public wherever they happen to be. If they are traveling in a bus or a truck, the vehicle stops at the proper time. On Fridays, which is the Muslim sabbath, men pray in a mosque.

The third pillar of Islam is charity. Muslims are expected to give 2.5 percent of their wealth to the poor every year.

The fourth pillar is fasting. Muslims are not supposed to eat, drink, or use tobacco between dawn and dusk during the holy month of Ramazan (Ramadan in Arabic), the ninth month of the Islamic calendar. The only exceptions to this rule are infants, people who are old or sick, nursing mothers, and pregnant women. Ramazan is considered holy because it is the month in which Muhammad received his revelations from God.

The fifth pillar is *hajj*, or pilgrimage. Every Muslim who is healthy enough and wealthy enough is supposed to make a pilgrimage to Mecca once in his or her lifetime.

More than a million people gather in Mecca for the annual hajj.

The Messenger of God

Muhammad was born around 570 in Mecca, Saudi Arabia. In those years, the city was a center of international trade. It was also a religious center where Arab pilgrims gathered once a year.

Orphaned at the age of six, Muhammad was raised by an uncle. When he grew up, he worked as a camel driver. Later he became a rich merchant. Despite his wealth and a happy marriage, he was a troubled man. He did not like the drinking and gambling that he saw around him because they often led to bloodshed. He also wondered about the religious beliefs of the Jewish

and Christian traders he met in Mecca. They worshiped a single God, while the Arabs worshiped many gods.

Muhammad began to think about the nature of God and the way people ought to behave. He spent hours by himself in a cave on a hillside. In 610, while he was asleep in the cave, he had a revelation. The angel Gabriel appeared and ordered him to recite Allah's messages in the name of God. After three years of hesitation, Muhammad finally began to do so.

At first only a few people became Muslims. Gradually, however, more and more people adopted the new religion. This made the leaders of Mecca unhappy. They were afraid that their city's economy would be ruined because pilgrims would no longer come there. They were also afraid that Muhammad was becoming too powerful politically. Mecca's leaders began attacking Muslims. Finally, in 622, Muhammad and his followers left Mecca and went to the city of Yathrib, known today as Medina, or "the city of the prophet." This journey became known as the *hejira*, or flight (left). The year 622 became the first year of the Islamic calendar.

Muhammad turned out to be an excellent military and political leader. The army that he organized in Medina defeated a much larger Meccan army. In 630 Muhammad and his army captured Mecca itself and made it Islam's center. Soon after, some one hundred tribes from all over Arabia converted to Islam. Then they set out to conquer and convert other peoples. The Arab Empire eventually stretched from India to Spain.

Muhammad died in 632. Today Muhammad is the most common name for Muslim men throughout the world.

Islam has many other rules. For example, Muslims are encouraged not to drink alcohol or eat pork. They are supposed to keep their heads covered. Women are expected to dress modestly. A man is allowed to have four wives as long as he treats them equally.

Sunnis and Shi'ites

When Muhammad died in 632, he did not name anyone to succeed him as leader of the Islamic community. As a result, his followers soon split into two groups. The Sunnis believed that the elders of the Islamic community should elect a successor from Muhammad's companions. The Shi'ites believed that the successor should be a member of Muhammad's family.

At present, about 80 percent of Afghanistan's Muslims are Sunnis. The Shi'ite minority consists mostly of such ethnic groups as the Hazaras and the Qizil Bash.

Sufis

Over the centuries, some Muslims felt the need for a more personal God. They formed groups called Sufi brotherhoods and tried to draw closer to God through such means as meditation, chanting, dancing, and drugs. Many Sufis wrote mystical poems that were passed on orally from father to son.

There are several Sufi orders in Afghanistan today. The leaders of two of these orders played important roles in the mujahedin resistance to Soviet occupation.

Religious Beliefs **93**

A mullah holds out a copy of the Koran.

A boy studies the Koran.

The most important clerics in Afghanistan are the mullahs. Each mullah is in charge of a mosque. There are 15,000 mosques in the country, one in almost every village and several in each city.

Every Friday at noon, the mullah delivers a sermon. He also runs the mosque school, where boys aged five to nine study the Koran and learn a little reading, writing, and arithmetic. The mosque school is often the only school in the village.

Most mullahs have a limited education. As a result, they often tend to be extremely conservative. They do not want any changes—such as education for women—in the traditional way of life.

Along with Islam, many Afghans believe in the supernatural. In their eyes, much of what happens in the world is controlled by evil spirits called bad *jinns*. There are several ways to protect yourself against a bad jinn. You can repeat certain phrases. You can wear an amulet or talisman. You can hang a piece of colored cloth on a pole near the village shrine. The shrine may be a pile of stones, a spring of water, a cave, or a tree. Some villagers believe that each shrine is inhabited by a holy being who protects the village, cures the sick, and gives people many children.

An Afghan woman kisses a pole as a sign of blessing at a shrine in Kabul.

An Active Culture

THE AFGHANS LOVE LANGUAGE. THEY HAVE ALWAYS HAD great poets and storytellers. They are also known for their architecture and sculpture. Music and dance play an important part in their everyday lives.

Opposite: **Afghanistan is a country that values its native literature.**

Literature

Afghanistan has been called a "nation of poets." Afghan literature consists mostly of spoken poetry. Afghans memorize poems and recite them in teahouses. Each clan, or group of related families, has a person who recites poems about the clan's history at weddings and other major events. These poems often deal with bravery in battle. Other popular themes include love, honor, family ties, and religion.

The best-known poets in the Pashto language are Kushal Khan Khattack and Abdur Rahman Baba. Both lived in the 1600s. A great military leader, Kushal Khan Khattack is considered Afghanistan's national poet. One of his works criticizes people who quote religious rules but do not behave properly:

The knowing, the perceptive man
Is he who knows about himself,
For in self-knowledge and insight
Lies knowledge of the Holiest.
If in his heart there is no fear,
His deeds are not those of the good.
Pay no heed to one who's skilled
In quoting the Koran by heart.

This red and silver cloth depicts Leila and Majnun

Stories about animals and tragic love stories make up most of the literature in the Dari language. *Kalilah wa Dimnah* is a collection of animal stories, each with a moral. These stories resemble Aesop's fables. The most famous love story is "Leila and Majnun." There are two versions. According to one version, Leila and Majnun are childhood playmates. When they grow up, they fall in love. Unfortunately, Majnun has no money, so Leila's father refuses to let them marry. Instead, Leila has to marry a rich man she does not love. Majnun goes mad with grief and wanders into the desert to live with the animals. Returning home years later, he learns that Leila's husband is dead. Now the two lovers can marry! When Leila and Majnun meet, however, they find that they have grown apart. Majnun returns to the desert, where he dies of a broken heart. Without anything to live for, Leila dies, too.

Architecture

Afghanistan's main contribution to architecture is its mosques, especially the Blue Mosque in Mazar-i-Sharif and the Friday Mosque in Herat. A Friday mosque is found only in towns with a population of more than 50,000. In addition to preaching sermons, the local mullah gives political information and advice to his congregants. Both the Blue Mosque and the Friday Mosque were built during the Timurid period.

The Blue Mosque is a particularly fine example of Timurid architecture. It has twin domes and several minarets, or towers. Each minaret has a walkway below its top where a *muezzin*

The Blue Mosque

stands to call people to prayer. The walls of the mosque are covered with pieces of glazed tile that form patterns of stems, leaves, and flowers. The tiles are mostly varying shades of blue, with a few white, green, yellow, and black tiles for contrast.

The Friday Mosque is noted for its marble courtyard, which is surrounded by arcaded walls. In the center of each wall is an open-fronted hall covered with tiles. A huge bronze cauldron, or large kettle, stands in the center of the courtyard. At one time the cauldron contained *sherbat*, a sweet drink that worshippers drank on feast days. Today, people use the cauldron as a place to put their donations.

Sculpture

Until very recently, Afghanistan boasted two of the world's largest statues of the Buddha. They stood in two niches cut into the sandstone cliffs near Bamian. The niches were about one-quarter of a mile (0.4 km) apart. The taller of the two statues towered 180 feet (55 m), or about the height of an 18-story building. The shorter statue stood 112 feet (34 m) high. The features of both statues were made from a mixture of mud and wheat straw that had been covered with painted plaster and then gilded. The taller Buddha wore a red cloak; the smaller Buddha, a blue cloak.

About 250 years ago, Nader Shah chopped off the legs of the larger Buddha. Some time later, fundamentalist Muslims

Partially destroyed statue of Buddha in Bamian

sawed off parts of the statues' faces. In March 2001, the Taliban ordered that the two statues be blown up with gunpowder. Only a few fragments remain.

For the Taliban, this act was a blow against idol worship. For many Afghans, the act meant the destruction of part of their history. Since 2001, an international group of architects, art historians, and museum curators have mounted an effort to reconstruct the statues.

Music and Dance

Afghans love to sing. Sometimes young men sing individually as they work. In the evening, they often get together in small groups to sing. In rural areas, the songs differ from one ethnic group to another. In the cities, the songs resemble those of India.

A traditional Afghan band contains either three or four musicians. One plays two small drums called *tabla*. The second plays a hand-pumped organ known as an Indian harmonium. The third plays a stringed instrument, such as the seventeen-stringed *rebab*. If there is a fourth musician, he plays a wind instrument. Traditional bands generally perform at weddings and festivals.

Traditional musicians play at a wedding.

The most popular Afghan dance is a war dance called the *attan*. Twenty to one hundred men dance in ever-widening circles around a fire or a stake. The older men are in the center, while the younger men are on the outside. The dancers swing guns or swords in their right hands, keeping the fire or stake on their left. The music starts slowly and gradually increases in speed. After reaching a climax, it stops. Then, after a short break, it starts up again. An attan may continue for hours.

At weddings, men and women dance in separate rooms. They do not dance with partners. Sometimes a row of twelve or so people will dance at the same time. Usually, however, only one person dances. When he or she sits down, another person gets up.

An Afghan family enjoys the dancing of one of its members.

The Cinema

Afghanistan's oldest film production company, Afghan Film Studio, was established by King Muhammad Zahir Shah, with support from Hollywood. At first the company made about twelve films a year. Then the Taliban closed it down. Now it is trying to resume business.

As of December 2002, only one film was being produced in Afghanistan. It is a collaboration between Afghan Film Studio and an Iranian company, Makhmalbaf Film House. The director is an Iranian woman named Samira Makhmalbaf. The film, which has not yet been given a title, deals with the role of women in a post-Taliban society. "Whenever I make a film," Makhmalbaf says, "my focus is to bring about a change for the better—particularly for women."

Makhmalbaf says that her biggest challenge in making the film was finding Afghan women willing to accept roles in it. When she sent out a casting call over Kabul TV, fewer than ten women showed up to audition. Makhmalbaf was told that she would have to bring an actress from Iran to play the lead. She refused: "I can't make a film about Afghanistan with an Iranian woman. I'll find her." After several weeks of searching, she finally found her lead: a student at Kabul University. First, however, the girl's parents had to read the script and be convinced that the film would not be full of music and love like an Indian movie.

In addition to coproducing Makhmalbaf's film, Afghan Film Studio is planning another film called *Rainbow*. The story of a girl who resists the Taliban, it will be written and

Samira Makhmalbaf

directed by Siddiq Barmak, who was the head of Afghan Film Studio when the Taliban closed it down. At that time, the Taliban also ordered that all existing reels of film be publicly burned. However, Barmak's colleagues managed to save their company's collection of newsreels, feature films, and historical footage. They placed the material in a storage room. Then they concealed the door to the room with a wall-sized screen, which they covered with Islamic posters.

The birth of an Afghan baby calls for three days of celebration, especially if the baby is a boy. Relatives fire guns and beat drums. Food is often given to the poor by the family.

The third day is the naming day. First the mullah whispers "*Allah-o-Akbar* [God is Great]" in the baby's ears. Then the mullah whispers the baby's name. In rural areas, the name is chosen by a paternal uncle. In urban areas, the name is chosen by the baby's parents. The mullah also tells the baby about its ancestors and urges it to be a good Muslim.

A newborn Afghan baby

A boy is considered a man when he reaches the age of seven. He is circumcized and puts on a cap or turban, which he will wear from then on. A girl is considered a woman when she is ten.

Becoming a man in Afghanistan means working hard.

Marriage Customs

Afghans usually marry at the ages of 18 to 20 for men and 16 to 18 for women. In urban areas, people often arrange their own marriage. In rural areas, however, marriages are arranged by the respective families. The groom's family pays a brideprice consisting of livestock, money, or both. The bride's family pays a dowry consisting of clothing, bedding, and other household goods. The groom's family usually pays for the wedding.

In many cases, weddings last for three days. On the first day, the bride's family visits the groom's house. On the second day, the groom, riding on a horse, leads a procession of musicians and dancers to the bride's house. On the third day, a

The groom's mother throws candy over the bride and groom to bring them the best of luck.

feast is held at the groom's house. That evening, the groom picks up his bride at her house and takes her back to his house for the official ceremony.

At the ceremony, the groom sits on one of two chairs that have been placed on a platform. The bride enters the room and moves very slowly toward the second chair. As she inches along, a band plays the wedding song, *Austa Biro*, or "Go Slowly," while the guests clap and sing, "Go slowly. Go slowly. Oh, bride, go slowly." When the bride is seated, a reddish brown paste called henna is smeared on the couple's hands. The marriage contract is signed and the mullah reads excerpts from the Koran. When the ceremony ends, guests throw sugared almonds and money at the couple so that they will have good luck and many children.

Death Customs

When an Afghan dies, the body is bathed by relatives—male relatives for a man, female relatives for a woman. A mullah recites prayers while the body is being bathed. After the toes have been tied together, the body is covered with a white shroud.

Burial always takes place in daytime. The corpse is buried on its right side, facing Mecca. For the next year, family members say prayers for the dead person every Thursday night. The women of the family wear white as a sign of mourning. It is considered bad luck to remove a plant from the graveyard. Many Afghans believe that doing so will either release an evil spirit or bring about another death in the family.

Lifestyles

T HE AFGHAN WAY OF LIFE IS BASED ON THE FAMILY, THE tribe, and Islam. Births, marriages, and deaths are major social occasions. The position of women is quite different from that in the United States. Education is limited. Sports and games are very popular, and Afghans play hard to win.

Opposite: **The family is highly valued in Afghanistan.**

The Family and the Tribe

The typical Afghan family is headed by the oldest male. He has complete control over the household. When the father dies, authority passes to the oldest son. When a son marries,

The oldest male is considered the head of the family.

he brings his bride to his parents' house. When a daughter marries, she goes to live in the house of her husband's family.

Members of a family consider themselves responsible for one another's well-being. If you fall ill or lose your job, you can always count on your family for help. Younger family members care for widows and the elderly. Property is owned jointly, and everyone contributes their earnings to a common pool.

Extended families include one's uncles, aunts, and cousins. An extended family may have as many as 100 members. The family's houses are generally clustered close together. People socialize within their extended family. They do a lot of visiting and often spend the night. Afghans prefer to marry a cousin.

Afghanistan's tribes are likewise headed by a male. Known as the *khan*, he usually belongs to the tribe's most aristocratic family. He is responsible for protecting the tribe's members and for settling disputes. A local jirga decides important matters. After everyone has expressed his opinion, the jirga reaches a common opinion that everyone is expected to follow.

The Position of Women

Before the twentieth century, Afghan women were generally regarded as property. Their place was in the home. They did not attend school. They were expected to obey their fathers or their husbands and to ask their permission to do most things. Women were not supposed to meet or talk with any man who

A Great Queen

At times in the country's past, Afghan women have played a strong public role. One example is Queen Gawhar Shad of Herat. During the 1400s, the Timurid kingdom of Herat stretched from China to Iraq. Although Gawhar Shad's husband held the title of emperor, he was a very weak man, and historians agree that the queen was the real ruler.

Gawhar Shad was a great patron of the arts. Her court attracted dozens of architects, artists, philosophers, and poets. She was responsible for the construction of a magnificent group of buildings that included a mosque, a college, and a mausoleum. After her husband died in 1447, she ruled by herself for ten years. She was murdered at the age of eighty. For years afterward, Afghan women made pilgrimages to her tomb in Herat and left gifts there.

was not a family member. If they went out of the house, they had to cover themselves with a veil. This was especially true of Pushtun women. Tajik, Hazara, and nomadic women had a little more freedom.

Under King Amanullah, in the 1920s, women were allowed to leave off their veils. "Religion does not require women to veil their hands, feet, and faces," the king said. "Tribal custom must not impose itself on the free will of the individual." The king's action infuriated religious and conservative Afghans. It was one of the main reasons for Amanullah's downfall.

Women gained more rights after Mohammad Daoud became prime minister in 1953. They were encouraged to take jobs outside the home. In 1959, they were allowed to enroll at Kabul University. Women received the right to vote in 1965. Before and during the Soviet occupation, many middle-class and urban women became teachers, doctors, and government workers.

The situation changed drastically when the Taliban came to power in 1994. Girls were expelled from school. Women were fired from their jobs. They were not allowed to use lipstick or nail polish or even to laugh out loud. Wearing a burka became compulsory. If a woman was caught walking alone in public, she was beaten.

"One night my grandmother was sick so I went to the pharmacy for medicine," said 28-year-old Humaira. "There

Shopping at an open market

were no men in our house so I had to go alone. The Taliban police caught me and yelled, 'How dare you go out without a male escort?' I explained. They lashed me anyway, across the back and legs, with thick wire cable. It hurt. But I went to the pharmacy all the same."

After the fall of the Taliban, many of the restrictions against women were lifted. Today, women are allowed to go to school and to hold jobs. Wearing a burka is no longer compulsory. Nevertheless, many women, particularly in rural areas, continue to shroud themselves in public. Many Afghan men still say that women should not be educated. An Afghan woman who runs away from an abusive husband is thrown in jail. So is a woman who refuses to marry the man her family has chosen for her.

A schoolteacher in Kabul

Men eat a meal with plenty of naan at hand.

The staple food of the Afghan diet is a round, flat loaf of unleavened bread called *naan*. It measures about 15 inches (38 cm) across and is either baked in an oven or fried on a griddle. Naan is usually made from wheat, although other grains are also used. Most Afghans, except in the larger cities, use a piece of naan as a plate for their meals.

The second most common food is rice. Rice is usually mixed with vegetables and, if people can afford it, meat. The most common vegetables are cabbage, carrots, cucumbers, eggplant, onions, potatoes, rhubarb, spinach, squash, and turnips. The main meat is lamb.

A well-known Afghan dish is *khormah*, lamb fried with vegetables. Kebabs are another favorite food. These are small chunks of lamb that have been threaded on a skewer with onions and tomatoes and then grilled.

Fresh fruits are plentiful in late summer. Grapes and melons are particularly tasty. Grapes are often dried in the sun to produce raisins. Other fruits include apples, apricots, cherries, figs, mulberries, peaches, pears, and plums.

A favorite dessert is *jelabi*, or fried rings of dough covered with syrup and molasses. Strong tea is usually served with each meal. Afghans drink two kinds of tea—green tea north of the Hindu Kush, and black tea in the south. They love to snack on nuts. Children drink goat's milk; adults eat yogurt and cheeses.

This vendor has a good selection of fruits and vegetables.

Making *Haft Miwa* or "Seven Fruits" Soup

In a bowl, mix one cup each of skinned almonds, skinned pistachios, and skinned walnuts. In a second bowl, mix one cup each of apricots, dried peaches, green raisins, and red raisins. Add 3 cups of cold water to each bowl and stir the mixtures thoroughly.

Then cover the bowls and put them in the refrigerator for two days. On the third day, mix the contents of the two bowls together, stir thoroughly, and start serving.

Haft Miwa is served only during the holiday of Nowruz.

Changing Fashions

The traditional national dress of Afghanistan consists of two garments worn by both men and women. One garment is a pair of extremely baggy trousers tied at the waist with a string. The second garment is a shirt that falls below the knees. Many women wear a long-skirted dress over their trousers. Men often wear vests. When the weather turns cold, men add a heavy sheepskin coat to their outfits, while women cover themselves with a warm wool shawl.

Some Afghan men wear caps made of karakul skin. Others wind a length of cotton cloth around a skullcap to make a turban. You can usually tell a man's ethnic group by the way his turban is tied. Men use their turbans for other purposes besides covering their heads. For example, they may use the length of cloth to drop a pail down a well. If a man dies away from home, his turban serves as a shroud.

After Taliban rule ended, men's clothing styles changed. Many men, especially in Kabul, adopted Western-style suits. As one man explained, he needed a suit in order to go to Korea

Most traditional clothing is made of cotton.

for his export-import business. "In other countries 85 percent of the people wear suits, and if we want to do business with them we have to wear suits too."

Women's clothing styles also loosened up after Taliban rule ended. Women in Kabul and other cities replaced their burkas with scarves that left their faces uncovered. In rural areas, however, women still wear the burka. "This is tradition for us," explained one woman.

The Taliban required men to have beards at least 4 inches (10 cm) long. This was particularly hard on Hazara men, who do not have much facial hair. When Taliban rule ended, one of the first things that many Afghan men did was rush to the local barbershop to have their beards either trimmed or shaved off.

A young Afghan woman shows her face, while others remain covered in post-Taliban Afghanistsan.

This dome-roofed village is in western Afghanistan.

Housing

Afghan cities are filled with five-story apartment and office buildings made of baked brick, concrete, or both. Some buildings in Kabul are thirteen stories high. Private homes have two stories. There are many supermarkets and other stores. Water is limited, however, and the plumbing systems do not always work.

Afghan villages consist of a series of enclosed compounds. Each compound houses a family. The houses and compound walls are built from bricks that have been baked in the sun and then plastered with a mixture of mud and straw. The roofs are usually flat and are made of reed matting covered with clay. Afghans have to re-mud the roof every fall to prevent it from leaking during the winter. They also have to shovel it free of snow so that it will not collapse. In summer Afghans use their flat roofs for sleeping and for drying fruits and vegetables. In some areas in the north and west, houses have domed roofs. In addition to a house, each compound usually contains some storage sheds, a stable for livestock, a cooking oven, a well, a garden, and an outhouse. Each compound is a world unto itself.

Village houses are simply furnished. People sit on cotton mats placed along the edges of a room. They eat on cotton cloths placed on the floor. At night they sleep on cotton mattresses that are piled in a corner during the day. Grain is stored in earthenware pots. Clothes, utensils, and weapons are kept in wooden chests.

Many Afghan nomads live in frameless tents woven out of black goats' hair. Seminomads, who spend part of the year farming, live in tents made of felt on a framework of wood.

The absence of frames makes it easy for nomads to put up and take down their tents.

In the past, the only schools in Afghanistan were religious schools run by mullahs. Only boys could attend. They learned to read the Koran and to chant it aloud. Because the Koran is written in the same script as Pashto and Dari, students also learned how to read one of the nation's two official languages. Sometimes the mullahs taught a little arithmetic. The school day was short, usually only three hours a day. Because most schools lacked heat, students took a three-to-four-month vacation every winter.

King Habibullah established Afghanistan's first public school in 1903. The curriculum included secular subjects as well as religion. Under Habibullah's successor, Amanullah, the public school system was expanded. Several high schools were opened, and a training college for teachers was set up. The year 1924 marked the opening of the country's first school for girls.

In 1931, elementary education became compulsory for boys and girls between the ages of seven and fifteen. Only a limited number of elementary schools were actually built, however. Even when there was a school, not everyone came to class. Children were expected to help their parents in the fields.

Education expanded after World War II. More elementary schools were built, including some for girls. The University of Kabul was founded in 1946. Vocational schools provided training in such subjects as business, home economics, secretarial services, tailoring, and nursing. Later the school curriculum expanded to include geography, history, and science.

Under the Soviet occupation, communist philosophy and the Russian language were included in the curriculum. Thousands of high school students were sent to study in the Soviet Union. The Soviets imported several university professors. The years of warfare severely damaged Afghanistan's educational system, however. Many schools were destroyed. Tens of thousands of teachers fled the country.

Under the Taliban, the school curriculum changed again. Religious classes took up half the day. Most science classes were outlawed. Girls were forbidden to attend school. Because all women teachers were fired from their jobs, the classroom size for boys rose as high as 200. The remaining male teachers could not handle that many students at one time. Even though boys attended school, they learned almost nothing. Despite the Taliban's rules, a few Afghan women ran secret schools for girls in their homes. If a suspicious Taliban official appeared, the students hid their books under the carpet.

After the Taliban fell, the new interim government reopened schools and promised to emphasize education. The school system still faces overwhelming problems, however. For one thing, less than one-third of Afghanistan's children are even enrolled in classes. The male literacy rate is currently under 50 percent, while the female literacy rate is under 10 percent.

Female students face special problems. A girl like Nazifa, who was in sixth grade when the Taliban closed her school, is still in sixth grade six years later. Moreover, she has forgotten almost everything she knew. "We are trying our best to recover the lost years," said teacher Maliha Jan, "but we don't

Afghan students struggle to learn under difficult conditions.

know how. All we can do is try." Many Afghans in rural areas do not want their daughters to go to school at all.

School buildings are in terrible condition. They lack desks, chairs, and chalkboards. Many students do not have textbooks, pens, or paper. There is no water, and toilets do not flush.

Playing Sports and Games

Afghanistan's national sport is *buzkashi*, or "goat pulling." It dates back to the days of Genghis Khan. Originally it was played with the headless carcass of a goat. Today players use a beheaded calf.

There are two teams of ten to twenty horsemen. At the starting signal, the men gallop toward the ditch where the dead animal has been placed. The idea is to lean down from the saddle, grab the carcass, ride down the field, reverse course and ride up the field, and drop the animal into a scoring circle. During this time, the members of the opposing team try to snatch the carcass away. Whichever team scores the most drops wins.

The playing field can be anywhere from 100 yards (91 m) to three miles (4.8 km) long. The carcass weighs about 150 pounds (55.9 kilograms). A rider often holds his horse's reins with his teeth, leaving his hands free to grab the carcass or to whip his horse. Pulling a rider of the opposing team off his horse is no longer allowed.

An official buzkashi game usually lasts one hour, with a ten-minute break at half-time. An unofficial game continues until both horses and riders are exhausted. Uzbeks are considered Afghanistan's best buzkashi players.

Many Afghan men compete in kite fighting, especially in Kabul and other cities. They maneuver their kites back and forth so as to break the string of an opponent's kite and cut it loose. Most kite fighters "glass" their strings by soaking them in a mixture of ground glass and paste. When the mixture dries, it leaves a jagged surface on the string. That makes it easier to cut someone else's kite string. Other Afghan sports include soccer, wrestling, and hunting.

Afghan children play games resembling hopscotch, marbles, and hide-and-seek. Toys include slingshots for boys and dolls for girls. Dolls are made from the stalks of the yarrow bush. Older boys play games that resemble soccer and cricket.

Thousands of Afghans watch a game of buzkashi.

Some engage in bird fighting. Fighting birds include larks, partridges, and roosters. The fight ends when one of the two opposing birds is killed.

Celebrating Holidays

Perhaps the happiest holiday in Afghanistan is Nowruz. This holiday occurs on the first day of the New Year, which is also the first day of spring. Afghans celebrate Nowruz on March 21. The holiday dates back some 2,500 years to the time when Zoroastrianism was practiced across much of central Asia.

Many Afghans celebrate Nowruz with an open-air fair. Carnivals run merry-go-rounds, Ferris wheels, and other rides.

Young Afghan children swing on a merry-go-round during Nowruz festivities in Kabul.

Children buy noisemakers. Adults play games of chance. Street vendors sell fried fish, boiled eggs, and pretzels dripping with honey. Some Afghans dye their livestock. You might see purple sheep and green chickens.

A special Nowruz ceremony is held at Mazar-i-Sharif. A flag is raised at the tomb of Hazrat Ali, son-in-law of the Prophet Muhammad. The flag is flown for forty days. During this time, thousands of pilgrims visit Mazar-i-Sharif. Some come to gain merit. Those who are sick or crippled come hoping for a cure.

Another important holiday is the religious festival of Eid-i-Ramazan (known in Arabic as Eid-ul-Fitr). It marks the end of the month of Ramazan, when most Muslims are required to fast from dawn to dusk. Afghans usually celebrate Eid-i-Ramazan for three days. They visit friends and relatives and eat special food. Children wear new clothes.

Another religious festival is Eid-i-Qurban (Eid-ul-Azhar in Arabic), which lasts four days. On the last day, people sacrifice an animal, usually a sheep. This marks a well-known religious event. God commanded Abraham to sacrifice his son Isaac. At the last minute, the angel Gabriel appeared and told Abraham to sacrifice a sheep instead. This story dramatizes the Muslim belief that you have to obey God's will without question.

National and Religious Holidays

Nowruz	March 21
Revolution Day	April 27
Workers' Day or Labor Day	May 1
Independence Day	May 27
Republic Day	July 17
Pushtunistan Day	August 31
United Nations Day	October 24

The dates of the following religious holidays vary from year to year:

Ashura, or Martyrs' Day

Mawlud-e-Sharif (the birthday of Muhammad)

Timeline

Afghan History

Afghans practice farming and herding.	6000 B.C.E.
Afghans live in small towns.	3000 B.C.E.
Indo-Aryans enter Afghanistan.	1500 B.C.E.
Zoroastrianism is introduced.	About 600 B.C.E.
The Persians conquer Bactria.	About 540 B.C.E.
Alexander the Great invades Afghanistan.	329 B.C.E.
The Mauryas conquer southern Afghanistan. Buddhism is introduced.	304 B.C.E.
Bactrian Greeks take over most of Afghanistan.	185 B.C.E.
The Kushans conquer Afghanistan.	About 130 B.C.E.
Arabs invade Afghanistan; Islam is introduced.	652
Mahmud of Ghazni reigns.	998–1030
The Mongols invade under Genghis Khan.	About 1221
The Golden Age of peace and prosperity occurs under the Timurids.	1370– about 1470
Babur reigns.	1504–1530

World History

2500 B.C.	Egyptians build the Pyramids and the Sphinx in Giza.
563 B.C.	The Buddha is born in India.
A.D. 313	The Roman emperor Constantine recognizes Christianity.
610	The Prophet Muhammad begins preaching a new religion called Islam.
1054	The Eastern (Orthodox) and Western (Roman) Churches break apart.
1066	William the Conqueror defeats the English in the Battle of Hastings.
1095	Pope Urban II proclaims the First Crusade.
1215	King John seals the Magna Carta.
1300s	The Renaissance begins in Italy.
1347	The Black Death sweeps through Europe.
1453	Ottoman Turks capture Constantinople, conquering the Byzantine Empire.
1492	Columbus arrives in North America.
1500s	The Reformation leads to the birth of Protestantism.

Afghan History

Ahmad Khan Abdali founds a dynasty that rules Afghanistan until 1973.	1747
Dost Muhammad Khan rules Afghanistan.	1818
The First Anglo-Afghan War occurs.	1838–1842
The Second Anglo-Afghan War occurs.	1878–1880
The Durand Agreement establishes Afghanistan as a buffer state between Russia and British India.	1893
The Third Anglo-Afghan War occurs; Afghanistan gains independence.	1919–1921
Muhammad Zahir Shah reigns.	1933–1973
Women vote for the first time in national elections.	1965
Mohammad Daoud seizes power and establishes a republic.	1973
The Soviet Union occupies Afghanistan.	1979–1989
A civil war is fought between the pro-Soviet government and the mujahedin.	1989–1992
The Taliban begins its rise to power.	1994
The United States hits the Taliban and terrorists in Afghanistan in retaliation for September 11, 2001, al Qaeda terrorist attack. An interim Afghan government is organized with Hamid Karzai at its head.	2001
The loya jirga establishes a transitional government.	2002

World History

1776	The Declaration of Independence is signed.
1789	The French Revolution begins.
1865	The American Civil War ends.
1914	World War I breaks out.
1917	The Bolshevik Revolution brings communism to Russia.
1929	Worldwide economic depression begins.
1939	World War II begins, following the German invasion of Poland.
1945	World War II ends.
1957	The Vietnam War starts.
1969	Humans land on the moon.
1975	The Vietnam War ends.
1979	Soviet Union invades Afghanistan.
1983	Drought and famine in Africa.
1989	The Berlin Wall is torn down, as communism crumbles in Eastern Europe.
1991	Soviet Union breaks into separate states.
1992	Bill Clinton is elected U.S. president.
2000	George W. Bush is elected U.S. president.
2001	Terrorists attack World Trade Towers, New York and the Pentagon, Washington, D.C.

Fast Facts

Official name: Islamic State of Afghanistan

Capital: Kabul

Official languages: Pashto and Dari

Kabul

Afghanistan's flag

Khyber Pass

Year of founding:	2002
Government:	Republic
Head of state:	President
Area and dimensions:	251,825 square miles (652,225 sq km)
Greatest distance north to south:	630 miles (1,012 km)
Greatest distance east to west:	820 miles (1,320 km)
Land borders:	Turkmenistan, Uzbekistan, and Tajikistan to the north; People's Republic of China to the northeast; Pakistan to the east and south; Iran to the west
Water borders:	None
Highest elevation:	Mount Nowshak, 24,557 feet (7,485 m)
Lowest elevation:	1,640 feet (500 m), in the Sistan Desert
Highest average temperature:	120°F (48.8°C)
Lowest average temperature:	24°F (-31°C)
Highest average annual precipitation:	53 inches (135 cm), in the east
Lowest average annual precipitation:	3 inches (8 cm), in the southwestern deserts

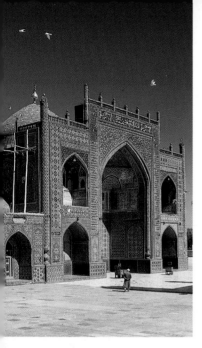

The Blue Mosque

Currency

National population (2001 est.):	26.8 million	
Population of largest cities (1988):	Kabul (2002 est.)	2,600,000
	Kandahar	225,500
	Herat	177,300
	Mazar-i-Sharif	130,600

Famous landmarks:
▶ *Blue Mosque*, Mazar-i-Sharif
▶ *Friday Mosque*, Herat
▶ *Tomb of Babur*, Kabul

Industry: Afghanistan's most important exports are opium and natural gas. The country also produces carpets and lapis lazuli. Some plants make cement, fertilizer, shoes, soap, and textiles.

Weights and measures: Afghanistan uses the metric system

Literacy: Men, under 50 percent
Women, under 10 percent

Currency: The afghani. Each afghani contains 100 puls. As of February 3, 2003, 42.7 afghanis were equal to U.S.$1.

Common words in Pashto:

lashkar	army
kitab	book
wor-kaey	child
bazgar	farmer
wuz	goat
astogna'h	home
safar	journey
zamin-dar	landowner

Afghan boy

Hamid Karzai

Local terms in Dari:

Shomaa chetaur hasted?	How are you?
Aaz amadan-e shomaa, khosh hastam.	I am glad that you have come.
Nam-e shomaa chist?	What is your name?
Khodaa haafez.	Goodbye.
Man na-mefahmam.	I do not understand.
Lotfat aasta boro!	Please drive slowly!
Tashnaab kojast?	Where is the washroom?
Che waqt ast?	What time is it?

Famous Afghans:

Mullah Muhammad Omar Akhund   (1959 or 1961–)
Leader of the Taliban

Babur   (1483–1530)
Conqueror of Afghanistan and founder of the Mogul Empire in India

Ahmad Khan Durrani   (1722–1773)
Founder of the kingdom of Afghanistan

Mahmud of Ghazni   (971?–1030)
Ghaznavid king

Hamid Karzai   (1957–)
Afghan president (2001–present)

Muhammad Zahir Shah   (1914–)
Last king of Afghanistan

To Find Out More

Books

▶ Ali, Sharifah. *Afghanistan*. New York: Marshall Cavendish, 1995.

▶ Ansary, Mir Tamim. *Afghanistan: Fighting for Freedom*. New York: Macmillan, 1991.

▶ Clifford, Mary Louise. *The Land and People of Afghanistan*. New York: J. B. Lippincott, 1989.

▶ Griffiths, John C. *The Conflict in Afghanistan*. Vero Beach, FL: Rourke Enterprises, 1989.

▶ Gritzner, Jeffrey A. *Afghanistan*. Philadelphia: Chelsea House, 2002.

Web Sites

▶ **Afghanistan**
encarta.msn.com
An account of the land, people, and culture.

▶ **Afghanistan**
www.cia.gov/cia/publications/factbook
Numerous facts about the country's geography, people, and government.

▶ **History of Afghanistan**
www.afghan-web.com
A survey of Afghan history.

▶ **History of Afghanistan**
www.afghanland.com
Historical survey, including material on art and architecture.

▶ **Culture of Afghanistan**
www.afghan-network.net
An account of the country's history and culture, with emphasis on such things as biographies and musical instruments.

Organizations

▶ **Republic of Afghanistan Embassy**
2341 Wyoming Avenue, NW
Washington, DC 2008

Index

Page numbers in *italics* indicate illustrations.

Meet the Author

IRIAM GREENBLATT writes books about history and other countries for children. Her publications include a junior high school history textbook as well as a series on rulers.

Greenblatt was asked to write about Afghanistan after completing a book on Iran for Children's Press. She did most of her research in the library at Highland Park, Illinois, where she lives, and in the library at Northwestern University in Evanston. She says, "If I had a question, I called Tamim

Ansary, an Afghan-American with whom I collaborated on a textbook on world geography and cultures. He always answered my questions right away." Statistics usually came from the Internet and *The New York Times*. Although Greenblatt has not visited Afghanistan, she spent several months in the neighboring nations of Iran, Uzbekistan, India, and the People's Republic of China.

Photo Credits